PRESIDENTIAL
RACES

PRESIDENTIAL
RACES

THE BATTLE FOR POWER IN THE UNITED STATES

ARLENE MORRIS-LIPSMAN

TWENTY-FIRST CENTURY BOOKS · MINNEAPOLIS

*To my husband Ed, with love and thanks for your encour-
agement, support, and computer skills*

*With my appreciation to the following, whose contributions
helped make this book possible: Marcia Marshall, my editor,
my Wednesday night colleagues in writing, the librarians at
Carnegie Main and Carnegie Squirrel Hill—Ben Tomek,
Kristen Bettcher, Nadine Dyga, and Larry Hokaj.*

Twenty-First Century Books
A division of Lerner Publishing Group, Inc.
241 First Avenue North
Minneapolis, MN 55401 U.S.A.

Website address: www.lernerbooks.com

Library of Congress Cataloging-in-Publication Data

Morris-Lipsman, Arlene.
    Presidential races : the battle for power in the United States / by Arlene
Morris-Lipsman.
        p. cm. — (People's history)
    Includes bibliographical references and index.
    ISBN 978–0–8225–6783–7 (lib. bdg. : alk. paper)
    1. Presidents—United States—Election—History—Juvenile literature.
2. Presidential candidates—United States—History—Juvenile literature.
3. Political campaigns—United States—History—Juvenile literature.
4. United States—Politics and government—Juvenile literature. I. Title.
E176.1.M923 2008
324.973—dc22   2006102637

Manufactured in the United States of America
1 2 3 4 5 6 – JR – 13 12 11 10 09 08

CONTENTS

*Decency required
that I should be so
entirely passive
during the . . .
contest.*

—Thomas Jefferson,
December 1800

LONG LIVE THE KING

UP...

Spring 2004. Democratic presidential nominee, John Kerry, motions to the crowd for silence, then addresses it. Hundreds of miles away, the Republican contender, President George W. Bush, rouses his own band of supporters. Later, each man boards his plane, heading for his next engagement—a small town meeting, a noisy rally, or perhaps a chance to have his photo taken, a photo op. At family dinners or on the street, on radio talk shows or on the Web, voters talk about the candidates. All the while, cameras roll, echoing the promises, regurgitating the missteps. Long before party conventions and the once-traditional Labor

Day kickoff, Campaign 2004 is in your face all the time.

It wasn't always like this. In America's early days candidates did not go out among the public to solicit votes. Instead, their supporters spoke for them. Candidates modeled themselves after George Washington, who never campaigned. But Washington didn't have to run for office. A convention of state delegates meeting in Philadelphia, Pennsylvania, in 1787 had written a new set of American laws, the Constitution. Washington had been that gathering's pick to lead the country as its first president. Even George Washington, however, couldn't just take command of the government. He had to abide by the rules.

According to law, electors, people appointed by the states, would select the president and vice president. In 1788 only four of the thirteen states allowed their citizens to vote directly for electors. In some states, the legislatures alone chose electors. Other states used a combination of selection by the legislature and by the voters.

When the electors met on February 4, 1789, they chose twice, but

George Washington (standing, center) *did not run for the office of the president. He was elected by state delegates in 1787. Here he delivers his inaugural address before members of Congress in April 1789. This engraving is based on a nineteenth-century painting by Tomkins Harrison Matteson.*

they did not indicate which vote was for the chief executive and which was for the vice president. All sixty-nine cast a ballot for George Washington. With the highest tally, he won the presidency. John Adams of Massachusetts, with the second-highest total of thirty-four, accepted the vice presidency. Several other men received a smattering of votes. A messenger delivered the news of their victories to the winners.

By 1792 two different philosophies on the nature of governing had emerged. Each was represented by a newly formed political party. Federalists supported manufacturing and industry and represented the upper classes. They demanded a strong central government and a loose reading of the Constitution. This means they would decide what the laws of the Constitution mean in each situation. Both Washington and Adams were linked to the Federalists, though they both loathed political parties. They felt that the fighting between parties could cause chaos for the new country.

The Republicans, headed by Thomas Jefferson and James Madison, wanted strong state governments, a weaker federal one, and strict interpretation of the Constitution. They would carry out the laws exactly as they were written. The Republicans envisioned a nation of farmers and believed in the wisdom of the common man.

At the end of Washington's four-year term, America's leaders asked him to stay on. This time, all 132 electors, from fifteen states, selected him as the president. However, Republicans supported George Clinton of New York over Adams for the vice presidency. Still, with 77 votes, Adams retained his post.

In 1796 Washington declined a third term. For the first time in the country's history, two candidates with different political outlooks would compete in a presidential contest.

...AND RUNNING

The first step in the 1796 election was choosing the candidates. Federalist Party heads exchanged letters about possible choices and sometimes met in small groups to discuss their options. Finally, they chose John Adams to represent them, along with a running mate, Thomas Pinckney of South Carolina. Republican leaders favored Thomas Jefferson with Aaron Burr of New York as the vice-presidential candidate.

The two nominees did not face the voting public or even each other, and both kept quiet on the issues. In 1796 most people agreed that actively campaigning for the presidential office was demeaning. John Adams stayed on his farm in Quincy, Massachusetts. Thomas Jefferson remained at Monticello, Virginia.

Each man declared his disinterest in the contest. Both claimed to be reluctant to serve. As Jefferson wrote in a December letter to a friend, "I had retired after five and twenty years of constant occupation in public affairs. My name, however, was again brought forward without concert or expectation on my part: (on my salvation I declare it)."

Their countrymen, however, did discuss the issues of the day. One of these issues was the tax Congress had levied in 1791 on whiskey production. Farmers often made whiskey from their corn or rye crop and then sold it all over the country. They resented the tax, which cut into their profits. International affairs were another issue in the 1796 campaign. In Europe, France and Britain had declared war on each other. Angry over the United States' apparent support for France, British ships seized U.S. vessels and forced the sailors to serve in the Royal Navy. Britain also encouraged Native Americans to attack settlers along the frontier. Washington sent John Jay, Chief Justice of the United States, overseas to resolve these problems. Congress ratified the treaty Jay worked out in 1795, but Republicans felt that Jay and the treaty failed to accomplish U.S. goals.

The press, which reflected the parties, voiced the voters' concerns. Republican-sponsored papers, handbills, and pamphlets attacked "His Rotundity," John Adams, and called him a monarchist. They claimed that as president he'd be far too kingly for the United States. Federalist newspapers targeted Jefferson, saying he was an anarchist who would do away with the national government.

Jefferson's note to Adams told another story, however. "The public and the papers have been much occupied lately in placing us in a point of opposition to each other," he wrote. "I trust with confidence that less of it has been felt by ourselves personally."

Sixteen states took part in the voting, which occurred on different days in different states. Ten legislatures chose their electors, while six states permitted a popular election. John Adams edged ahead to win the presidency with seventy-one votes. Jefferson, trailing Adams by only three votes, became his vice president.

John Adams took the oath of office on March 4, 1797, in Philadelphia, which was the nation's capital at that time. Before his term ended though, he moved to Washington, D.C., the new permanent capital of the United States, and became the first president to live in the White House.

George Washington toasts incoming president John Adams at Washington's farewell dinner in 1797.

During Adams's term, France believed that the U.S. government sided with the British after the signing of the Jay Treaty. So France began to seize U.S. ships. The United States fought back in an undeclared war against France. Fearing open warfare, the Federalist Congress pushed through the Alien and Sedition Acts, which Adams signed. These acts allowed the president to deport foreigners he thought dangerous and to stifle any Republican criticism of the government.

The Republicans raged against the suppression of freedoms allowed in this new legislation. In this 1800 election year, the congressmen of each political party caucused, or met, to choose who would represent them. Federalists again named John Adams and running mate Charles Cotesworth Pinckney of South Carolina. Republicans stayed with Thomas Jefferson and Aaron Burr.

Still the candidates didn't openly campaign. As Thomas Jefferson remarked in December, "Decency required that I should be so entirely passive during the . . . contest." The electors decided it was time for a change and chose Jefferson. He received seventy-three electoral votes to Adams's sixty-five. Aaron Burr, however, also received seventy-three votes, the same number of votes as Jefferson. Since there weren't separate ballots for president and vice president, Burr and Jefferson were tied for president. By constitutional law, the House of Representatives would resolve such a deadlock. The representatives deliberated for six days and thirty-six ballots. Finally, on February 17, 1801, Thomas Jefferson won ten states—he needed nine—and the presidency. Three years later, Congress passed the Twelfth Amendment. Electors would thereafter vote separately for president and vice president. Upset over his loss, John Adams left the capital early and did not witness Jefferson's inauguration.

In 1804 the Republican caucus again chose Thomas Jefferson as its presidential candidate. The Federalist Party selected Charles Cotesworth Pinckney to represent it.

Thomas Jefferson let his record speak for him. He'd purchased the Louisiana Territory from France in 1803. With the purchase, the

United States gained control of a huge tract of western land and of the Mississippi River. The Federalists had few issues, few supporters, and barely campaigned. Thomas Jefferson won the contest in a landslide, 162 electoral votes to 14.

Like Washington, Jefferson stepped down after two terms. Fellow Virginians, James Madison and James Monroe, followed him, each serving eight years. Despite grumblings about the fairness of the caucus system, it continued to be used to choose the presidential and vice-presidential candidates, especially for the Republican Party. The Federalist Party was already starting to disintegrate and didn't always formally caucus. By the 1824 election, however, "King Caucus" was to be dethroned.

DEATH OF A CAUCUS

Our Founding Fathers extended voting privileges to white males who owned property. Eventually, nonlandholders (still white and male) obtained the right to vote. By the 1824 election, all but six states allowed all free male citizens to select the members of the Electoral College.

By 1820 the Federalist faction had completely fallen apart, leaving the country with a single party. James Monroe ran unopposed that year. In 1824 five contestants from the Republican Party pursued the presidency: John Quincy Adams of Massachusetts, William Crawford of Georgia, John Calhoun of South Carolina, Henry Clay of Kentucky, and Andrew Jackson of Tennessee. State legislatures had nominated four of the candidates, but Republican leaders meeting in caucus chose William Crawford as the party's legitimate nominee.

Only sixty-six men, however, one-third of Congress, had attended the February 14 session that selected Crawford. The other contenders complained that the caucus pick was unfair. As Andrew Jackson stated in a March 28, 1824, letter, "I am happy to see the good people of [A]merica are putting their faces against these congressional caucuses; & I do hope the one last held will put the unconstitutional proceeding to sleep forever—and leave to the people their constitutional right of free suffrage."

The candidates still did not actively campaign. "I never did electioneer, intrigue, or combine for office in my life," Andrew Jackson wrote in a letter dated March 25, 1824. "Could I in this way obtain one, even the most distinguished, the . . . honor of the post, would be lost in a recollection of the manner after which it was obtained."

The public learned about the candidates from the newspapers, and the nominees' correspondence often appeared in print. The news headlines of the day featured serious accusations. Murderer!—Andrew Jackson, for the military executions he'd ordered as an officer in the War of 1812. Mismanagement of office!—William Crawford, secretary of the treasury. Gambler!—Henry Clay. They found petty faults too. Sloppy dresser! A snob!—John Quincy Adams. Real concerns included the caucus system and the special interests of each section of the country. Mostly, though, the issue was personalities.

Four candidates seemed well qualified to fill the presidential office. John Quincy Adams, William Crawford, John Calhoun, and Henry Clay had spent years in government. Unlike them, Andrew Jackson was new to politics.

During the contest, William Crawford suffered from a stroke. Calhoun was named as a candidate for the vice presidency. Clay though offered voters a real program, the American System. This called for a tariff—a tax on imported goods—to protect U.S. industries and promote their growth. The American System urged improvements in transportation—more highways and canals—to open the West and to encourage trading among the states. It also pressed for a national bank in order to keep the currency sound. Most voters, however, deliberated between John Quincy Adams and Andrew Jackson.

During the race, Adams didn't care to state his positions. Jackson remained quiet on issues too, but his supporters released a first-ever campaign biography. The "Life of Jackson" reminded the public of

This political cartoon portrays the presidential race of 1824. A crowd of citizens cheers on presidential candidates (from left to right in front), *John Quincy Adams, William Crawford, and Andrew Jackson. Henry Clay* (far right in dark coat) *dropped out of the race.*

his military accomplishments. General Jackson and his troops had defeated the British in the Battle of New Orleans in 1815 at the end of the War of 1812. He'd faced off against the Creek Indians and later, the Seminoles in Florida.

Adams, at first, hoped Jackson would run as his vice president. "John Quincy Adams/Who can write/Andrew Jackson/Who can fight," shouted others who shared Adams's sentiments. But Jackson had no intention of being vice president. His eye was also on the top spot.

To the people, Old Hickory, as they nicknamed Jackson because of his toughness, was a hero. And with his western frontier background and lack of education, he seemed like a common man, despite being a wealthy landowner.

In the first election that tallied the popular count, Jackson received 43 percent of the popular vote and 99 electoral votes, followed by Adams (31 percent and 84 votes), Crawford (13 percent and 41 votes), and Clay (13 percent and 37 votes). Since Jackson had not received the necessary majority of electoral votes, 131, the House of Representatives would choose a winner from among the top three contenders.

Each of the twenty-four states cast one vote, and the winner needed thirteen to claim the presidency. Henry Clay, who had not qualified, sputtered his outrage. "I cannot believe that killing 2500 Englishmen at N. Orleans qualifies for the various difficult and complicated duties of the chief magistracy." He urged his supporters to select Adams.

John Quincy Adams won the presidency, even though he received fewer popular votes than Jackson, the first time this had ever occurred in an election. Several days later, Adams appointed Clay secretary of state.

"Corrupt bargain," Jackson and his followers insisted. They accused Adams and Clay of making a deal—Clay's votes for a spot in Adams's administration.

John Quincy Adams saw the situation differently. He wrote on February 9, 1825, "I attended . . . the drawing-room at the President's. It was crowded to overflowing. General Jackson was there, and we shook hands. He was altogether placid and courteous." Despite Adams's take, an angry Andrew Jackson split from the Republicans and declared his intention of running for the presidency in 1828.

Jackson's supporters in Congress challenged the president's agenda and enacted few of his proposals. Some of his programs, however, were put into effect. For instance, work was begun on two important canals—the Chesapeake and Ohio and the Delaware and Chesapeake. Since roads were poor throughout the country, most transportation was by boat. Canals connecting other bodies of water opened more areas of the country for trade and settlement.

During Adams's presidency, a small group of African Americans in New York produced the first black newspaper, *Freedom's Journal,* in 1827. Noah Webster published his first *American Dictionary of the English Language* (1828). Engineers broke ground for the Baltimore and Ohio, the country's first freight and passenger railroad in 1828. Mostly, though, Congress waited for 1828, when Andrew Jackson would take his revenge.

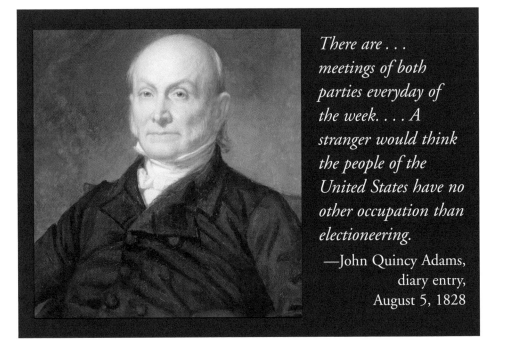

There are . . . meetings of both parties everyday of the week. . . . A stranger would think the people of the United States have no other occupation than electioneering.

—John Quincy Adams, diary entry, August 5, 1828

A ROUSING GOOD TIME

PEOPLE POWER

Andrew Jackson began his march to power in 1825 when the Tennessee legislature again nominated him as a presidential candidate. The caucus had lost all support and was finally dead. Jackson and his supporters formed a new party, the Democrats, and opposed Adams and his National Republicans.

The National Republicans wanted a strong central government. They also felt that a handful of educated statesmen should run the country. The Democrats favored less national rule and more emphasis on the rights of the individual states to determine their own laws.

They respected and listened to the voice of the common man.

In 1828, for the first time ever, voters actively participated in American politics. As John Quincy Adams noted in his diary on August 5, "In the evening there was a Jackson-party popular meeting in the square. . . . There was a similar meeting of the friends of the Administration a few nights since . . . and There are . . . meetings of both parties everyday of the week. . . . A stranger would think the people of the United States have no other occupation than electioneering."

Although Jackson directed his race from behind the scenes, he did not campaign. But the Democratic Party, with both national and state committees, led the public through a frenzy of activities.

For the Jacksonians, the contest centered on Jackson's nickname, Old Hickory. Hickory saturated the contest. Democrats planted hickory trees on street corners, swept with hickory brooms, carried hickory walking canes, wore hickory leaves in their caps, and even formed Hickory Clubs. Jacksonians hosted barbecues, dinners, rallies, and parades. For the first time during a campaign, a party offered the public souvenir bandanas, combs, sewing boxes, and ceramic pieces— all advertising the nominee.

Adams didn't campaign either, and the National Republicans ran a more subdued race. They didn't understand the Jacksonian antics. "Odds nuts and drumsticks," they said. "What have hickory trees to do with . . . the great contest?" Their questions didn't stop Jackson's Hurra Boys, his campaign workers.

That 1828 contest was fun. It was also dirty. Party newspapers on both sides fueled rumors and lies. Democrats denounced President Adams as a monarchist and an aristocrat. And the "corrupt bargain" he'd made with Clay in the 1824 election still haunted him.

The National Republicans charged Jackson with marrying his wife, Rachel, before her divorce from another man was final. This was true, but the couple hadn't known it. They accused him of being uneducated (true!) and said he challenged his enemies to duels, even killing some (true!). They also issued the "Coffin Handbill," which

This handbill, produced during the 1828 presidential campaign, opposed Andrew Jackson's bid for the U.S. presidency. It pictures six coffins representing the soldiers Jackson ordered shot for desertion. More coffins represent soldiers and Native Americans whom Jackson allegedly condemned and ordered executed during the War of 1812, while a woodcut portrays Jackson's stabbing of a man in Nashville.

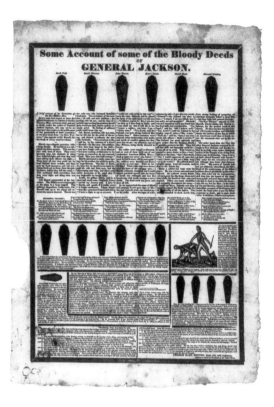

included "Some Account of Some of the Bloody Deeds of General Jackson." Six coffins, for the six militiamen Jackson ordered shot for desertion, decorated this flyer adorned in black.

In 1828 more average Americans went to the polls than ever before, and Jackson won. For the first time ever, a man known only for his military feats would head the country. But Jackson's victory was bittersweet. His wife died of a heart attack soon after the election. The general blamed John Quincy Adams and Henry Clay for allowing their supporters to humiliate her, which he believed caused her death.

After his defeat, John Quincy Adams noted in his diary (December 3), "The sun of my political life sets in the deepest gloom." He refused to attend Jackson's inauguration. Instead, he left Washington the night before the ceremony, as his father, John Adams, had done in 1800.

After his inaugural, Jackson threw the doors to the White House open. Mobs of citizens crammed into the mansion, stepped on furniture, soiled carpets, broke glass and china, and celebrated the victory.

Four years later, in time for Jackson's second bid for office, the national convention emerged on the scene, in response to the more democratic political climate. Each party sent delegates to their party's convention to select their candidate.

One party, the Anti-Masons, held the first-ever convention in September 1831 and nominated William Wirt of Maryland. Anti-Masons banded together to oppose Freemasonry, an international organization of upper-class men. Masons are an organization that uses secret signs

Crowds of president-elect Jackson's supporters thronged to the White House for his inauguration on March 4, 1829. This print was pubished in The Playfair Papers, or Brother Jonathan, the Smartest Nation in All Creation, *a three-volume work published in London in 1841.*

and rituals in their private meetings. Anti-Masons believed Freemasonry secrecy harmed democracy. The Anti-Masonic party was America's first time a third (minor) political party organized.

National Republicans held their convention in December 1831 and chose Henry Clay as their candidate. The Democrats met in May 1832. Delegates had already decided on Andrew Jackson, but they voted on a running mate, Martin Van Buren, Jackson's first choice.

In 1832 Jackson ran on his record, which included the Indian Removal Act. This legislation forcibly uprooted Native Americans—the Creek, the Choctaw, and the Cherokee—from the southeastern United States and sent them beyond the Mississippi River to the Territory of Oklahoma. It was a popular act because it freed Indian lands for white settlers. The Native American groups argued against it in court. Chief Justice John Marshall agreed that the Cherokee were entitled to their land. But Jackson enforced the law anyway, so the Native American were moved west along what came to be called the Trail of Tears.

The chief issue of the election centered on the Second Bank of the United States, which held federal deposits, awarded loans, and controlled America's economic interests. Jackson believed the bank looked out for wealthy Americans and ignored average citizens.

In 1816 Congress had granted the bank a twenty-year charter. In 1832, four years before that charter was to end, the bank's president asked for its renewal. Jackson vetoed a bill that would have rechartered it.

During the presidential race, Clay taunted Jackson, calling him King Andrew, the tyrant who wanted to control the government. Clay's followers also attacked Jackson in political cartoons, an effective and popular campaign tool.

Again, everyday Americans threw their support to Jackson. Governing his fellow citizens, Jackson, the first president born on the western frontier (in the Carolinas), had shown that he represented ordinary people and was obliged to follow their wishes. For the masses, used to being governed by the better-educated elite, this was a new, bewildering, and exhilarating idea.

One political cartoonist in 1833 depicted President Jackson as a king determined to rule without regard for democracy or the Constitution, which lies in tatters at his feet.

A FRENZY OF POLITICS

In 1834 Jackson's political enemies formed a party called the Whigs. During the Revolutionary War (1775–1783), Whigs had opposed the British king, just as these Whigs opposed Jackson. He stepped down after his second term. Martin Van Buren was nominated by the Democrats for the 1836 race. The recently organized Whig Party ran three candidates against Van Buren and lost. But Van Buren's running mate, Richard Johnson, did not receive a majority of votes for vice president from the Electoral College. Some southern electors objected to his open relationship with a black woman. In such cases, the Senate is required by law to select a vice president. It chose Johnson anyway.

By 1840 the Whigs had become a national party. That year

Democrats and Whigs staged the first modern campaign by appealing to ordinary citizens for support. In the 1840 campaign, Van Buren officially ran without a running mate. The Democratic convention refused to renominate Johnson because of the racial issues.

The Whigs chose William Henry Harrison, with John Tyler as his running mate. Harrison had caught the public's eye when he claimed victory over the Shawnee Indians in a battle near the Tippecanoe River in 1811. As one of the three Whig candidates, he'd lost in a run for the presidency in 1836, but he'd been a popular contender.

Early in the race, a Democratic newspaper had poked fun at Harrison, calling him Old Tippecanoe and noting that he would be happy to sit in a log cabin, sip cider, and receive a pension for the rest of his life. The Whigs used this put-down and proclaimed that Harrison was a cabin-dwelling, cider-sipping, ordinary man.

In fact, William Harrison didn't live in a log cabin. He owned a huge house in Ohio. He came from a wealthy old Virginia family, and his father had signed the Declaration of Independence.

The Whigs hoped to convince voters of their version of the story. Log cabins popped up everywhere—on banners and ribbons, on glasses and mugs, even on soaps and china plates. Americans passed the cider jug and drank to Harrison. The log cabin and the barrel of cider symbolized Old Tippecanoe, military hero and man of the people.

Everyday folks liked William Henry Harrison. They didn't like Martin Van Buren, or Van Ruin, as they called him. During Van Buren's term, the country had faced a financial depression. People believed the president drank champagne and lived a life of luxury, while they struggled through hard times. Van Buren, however, was more the common man than Harrison. His father had owned a country tavern, and Martin had worked his way up the political ladder to finally become president. Still, his critics jeered, "Van, Van, the Used Up Man."

In his autobiography, Van Buren would later write, "As far back . . . as Mr. Monroe's administration, a quantity of very extravagant French furniture was purchased for the Presidential mansion.

An 1840 Whig campaign ribbon for William Henry Harrison (left) portrays the candidate above a log cabin. The Whig Party pushed the log cabin association, even though Harrison wasn't raised in one, as a way to convince voters that he was a common man. The public swallowed the story and criticized Democrat Martin Van Buren for living a luxurious life. One of the few campaign prints issued in support of incumbent Van Buren (right) was designed to oppose this perception. The print touts Van Buren's executive order reducing the workday of federal employees to ten hours.

These . . . were still at the White House in my time. I was charged with having purchased them, and the alleged extravagance made matter of accusation against me."

In 1840 Van Buren did not campaign. Rather, he wrote letters to his allies, and some appeared in print. His fellow Democrats also stumped the country and spoke out for O. K. The president came from Kinderhook, New York, and was nicknamed Old Kinderhook or O. K. O. K. soon became a popular expression.

At first Harrison didn't campaign either. Whig leaders wanted their man quiet on issues and big on image. There were issues, though, especially economic ones. Democrats drafted the first-ever party platform—a statement of the issues they felt were important and on which they would campaign. "The federal government is one of limited powers, derived solely from the constitution," they wrote. And "congress has no power to charter a national bank."

Harrison's opponents accused him of being General Mum and mocked his silence. Then Old Tippecanoe stunned Americans. He toured a few areas of the country and spoke out. "I am fully aware, my fellow citizens," he said in a speech on September 10, "that you expect from me some opinion upon the various questions which now agitate our country. Calumny [Lies] . . . hath proclaimed that I am averse from declaring my opinions on matters so interesting to you; but nothing can be more false. Have I not . . . proclaimed my opposition to a citizen's going forward . . . and soliciting votes for the Presidency?" Harrison's enemies had accused him of not talking about issues. In this speech, he takes a stand on one: a candidate should not directly ask voters for their support!

It didn't matter to voters that Harrison rarely discussed issues of importance. Men and even women (although they couldn't vote) threw themselves into the frenzy of the Whig's celebrations, barbecues, and parades. Citizens sang dozens of log cabin songs, recited poems, and read about Harrison in the *Log Cabin*, a Whig newspaper. They enjoyed the floats with log cabins in the parades. Chanting the soon-to-become-popular refrain, "Keep the Ball A-Rolling," they gasped at huge balls of buckskin or tin that were rolled from town to town. And they shouted the slogan that would become one of the most memorable in campaign history, "Tippecanoe and Tyler Too."

As for the Democrats, they could only answer the question, "Will Harrison win?" with "Nosirrah," (*Harrison* spelled backward).

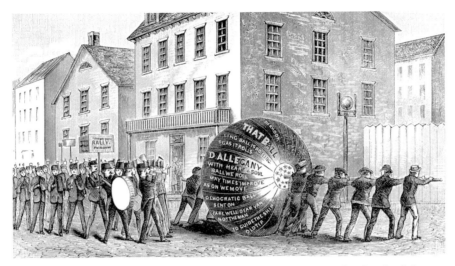

During a Harrison campaign rally, several men work to roll a big buckskin ball through the streets of town. The campaign that Harrison and the Whigs ran during the 1840 presidential election focused on slogans, songs, parades, and a party atmosphere. This was an innovative strategy for its time and set the stage on which future campaigns would be run.

Although they belittled Harrison and his military record, they couldn't compete against the Whigs. Neither could the third candidate who had entered the race, James G. Birney, representing the newly formed Liberty Party, which opposed slavery.

At last the merrymaking wound down. In the fall of 1840, more than 80 percent of those eligible cast their votes. Old Tippecanoe won the election. With Van Buren's defeat, the Whigs sang, "Farewell, dear Van/You're not our man/To guide the ship/We'll try old Tip."

On March 4, 1841, sixty-eight-year-old Harrison offered the nation his thoughts. The country's oldest president yet delivered the longest inaugural speech in U.S. history, almost two hours. Coatless and hatless, he braved the wind and bitter weather to speak to his countrymen. He caught a cold that developed into pneumonia. One month later, William Henry Harrison died, the first presidential death in office. Vice President John Tyler took over the presidency.

A house divided against itself cannot stand. I believe this government cannot endure, permanently half slave and half free. I do not expect the Union to be dissolved—I do not expect the house to fall—but I do expect it will cease to be divided.

—Abraham Lincoln, 1858

CONFRONTATIONS

ERUPTIONS

By his term's end, President Tyler was working to annex Texas (add it to the United States). In 1836 Texas had declared its independence from Mexico, which had originally owned it, and had asked to join the United States. Many, including southerners, delighted in the thought of expanding the nation's borders. This idea of expanding borders was soon to be called Manifest Destiny. Others, especially northerners, were not anxious to add Texas to the Union (United States) because it would be admitted as a state that allowed slavery. These voters were opposed to expanding slavery. Texas became the main issue in the 1844 presidential campaign.

For this contest, the Whigs chose the well-known Henry Clay. The Democrats, deadlocked for eight ballots in their convention, finally settled on James K. Polk. Polk became the nation's first dark horse candidate. In politics, a dark horse is someone who is not expected to be nominated but, as in a horse race, comes up from behind to win. The dark horse is usually a compromise choice. Of his nomination, Polk wrote on June 8, 1844, "I need scarcely say to you that the nomination for the Presidency was not anticipated by me. I have certainly never sought it, but if voluntarily conferred I will not decline it."

"Who Is James K. Polk?" the Whigs sneered. But in this campaign, issues mattered, not famous names. Although they both owned slaves, the nominees sidestepped that brewing controversy and focused only on annexation.

In 1844 Henry Clay didn't actively campaign, but newspapers published many of his letters. Worried about a possible war with Mexico over Texas, Clay came out against annexation. When that angered southerners, Clay backpedaled. That infuriated northerners.

In this political cartoon from the 1844 presidential race, the artist portrayed the candidates as faces on racehorses, each ridden by a supporter. Front-runners Henry Clay (far left) *and James Polk* (second from left) *lead the pack.*

James Polk didn't campaign, wrote few letters, and never spoke publicly. Still, he supported his party's stand on annexation. To offset the addition of Texas as a slave state, Democrats called for American control of all Oregon, a free territory. Up until that time, Britain and the United States shared the Oregon Territory up to the latitude of 54°40'. "Fifty-Four Forty or Fight," became a Democratic slogan.

Voters in twenty-six states headed for the polls to choose the Whig, Democrat, or even the Liberty Party ticket, which was again running James G. Birney. Only the Liberty Party pushed openly for abolition (doing away with slavery). Henry Clay lost the contest to Polk. Later, Clay said of his defeat, "I will not disguise . . . that I felt the severity of that blow . . . because . . . it was altogether unexpected by me."

Congress annexed Texas in February 1845, just before Polk took office. Mexico, unhappy with losing Texas, sent troops across the Rio Grande in 1846. They invaded what Polk claimed was U.S. territory and attacked U.S. soldiers. The president insisted that a state of war existed, and Congress finally agreed to finance the Mexican-American War (1846–1848). A victory by the United States led to the signing of a peace treaty. This treaty gave New Mexico (most of the present southwestern United States) and California to the victor. In the Northwest, Polk compromised with Britain on an Oregon boundary set at the 49° line of latitude, adding the Oregon Territory to the United States. Despite his winning record, Polk stepped down after a single term in office, as he had promised he would.

By 1848, with expansion accomplished, the slavery question nagged at Americans. They argued over whether slavery should be extended by congressional law into the newly acquired territories. This was the scorching issue in the next few presidential contests, as the two national parties scrambled to find candidates who could draw their northern and southern factions together.

In 1848 Democrats compromised on Michigan senator Lewis Cass. Cass was a doughface, one who sympathized with the South, although he hailed from the North. Angry Democrats (called Barnburners) who opposed Cass walked out of their convention. It was said they would "burn down the barn to oust the rats." They would destroy the party to be rid of the Hunkers, the delegates who supported slavery's extension.

The Whigs settled on General Zachary Taylor, a Mexican-American War hero and a Louisiana slaveholder who had never even voted. At this time, candidates were sent letters of notification informing them of their nominations. Taylor did not immediately receive his. He refused to pay the postage due, and his mail landed in the dead letter office!

Cass, Taylor, and their party leaders either offered vague statements about slavery or avoided the subject entirely. The Free Soil Party did not. Shouting "Free Soil, Free Speech, Free Labor, and Free Men," they nominated former president Martin Van Buren and opposed the extension of slavery into the territories.

Slavery was a central issue in the 1848 presidential campaign. Democrats who opposed their party's candidate (also known as Barnburners), Lewis Cass, on the issue of slavery formed their own Free Soil Party. One artist literally depicts Free Soil candidate Martin Van Buren and his son setting a barn on fire.

For the first time ever, Americans all voted on the same day, November 7, 1848. Before this election, the day had varied from state to state. Taylor won, but the Free Soil Party gained 10 percent of the popular vote, the largest tally yet for a third party.

In July 1850, Taylor fell ill with stomach pains and died in office. Vice President Millard Fillmore took over the presidency. The furor over slavery grew.

The nation had hoped that the slavery issue would be resolved with the enactment of the Missouri Compromise of 1820. According to it, Maine would enter the Union as a free, non-slave-owning state, while Missouri would come in as a slave state. This would keep the number of slave states and free states equal. In addition, the compromise forbade slavery in the rest of the Louisiana Purchase north of the 36°30' line of latitude.

By the end of the summer of 1850, because of the additional territories won in the Mexican-American War, Congress enacted another compromise, one that many hoped would be the final word on slavery. The Compromise of 1850 included the following provisions. California would be admitted to the Union as a free state. Utah and New Mexico were established as territories, and their settlers would decide for themselves whether to allow slavery. Slave trading was abolished in the District of Columbia. A new Fugitive Slave Law made it easier for southerners to press for a return of runaway slaves who found their way North. Both parties felt the compromise was the best they could do, considering the explosiveness of the slavery issue.

In 1852 Democrats chose the little-known Franklin Pierce of New Hampshire to represent them. For the first time, a notification committee visited the candidate to inform him of his nomination instead of sending him a letter.

Pierce followed tradition by staying home and keeping silent. The Whig candidate, however, General Winfield Scott, a Mexican-American War hero, traveled west on a "nonpolitical" tour to inspect sites for military hospitals. He didn't discuss politics, but he did

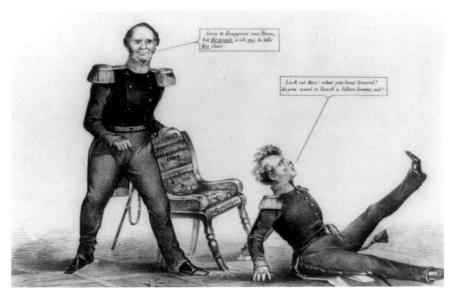

This political cartoonist anticipated a Whig victory in 1852, as Whig candidate Winfield Scott pulled the presidential chair out from under Democrat Franklin Pierce. Pierce routed Scott in the election.

address some crowds. His horrified enemies criticized his outlandish, undignified behavior.

Pierce toppled Scott, 254 electoral votes to 42, but Pierce began his presidency in personal tragedy. Just before his inauguration, Franklin Pierce watched as his young son was crushed to death in a train accident.

In 1854 the newly enacted Kansas-Nebraska Act allowed settlers in those territories to make their own decisions regarding slavery. Proslavery and antislavery forces fought in Kansas. Tempers raged even in Congress, where a proslavery South Carolina representative severely beat an antislavery Massachusetts senator with his cane. As for the Whig Party, internal conflict over slavery tore it apart and finally destroyed it. Founded just twenty years earlier, the party faded into history.

In 1856 Democrats, with the only national party remaining, chose James Buchanan as their candidate. But a new northern party, standing against the extension of slavery, had emerged in 1854. Calling itself the

A woodcut print from the 1856 presidential election shows voters (white male citizens) at the polling booths for the three candidates: James Buchanan (left), John Frémont (center), and Millard Fillmore (right).

Republican Party, it nominated former western explorer John Frémont.

The American Party, originally just a secret society formed in 1849, also ran a candidate in this election. The society originally formed to support candidates who favored its stands against Catholics and immigrants. When questioned about their group, members answered, "I know nothing about it." Like other parties, these Know Nothings split over slavery. The southern faction finally nominated former president Millard Fillmore. Fillmore won eight electoral votes (22 percent), the first time a third party received electoral votes.

By now the din over slavery enveloped the nation. Republicans crusaded against the barbarism of slavery. A large segment of the Democrats insisted on slavery's extension, and the South threatened to secede (leave the Union) if Frémont won. Amidst the turmoil, Buchanan won the election. By his term's end, however, the United States had begun its march toward civil war.

TRADITION...OR NOT

In 1860 four parties, each with its own agenda, ran presidential candidates. The Republican Party, which spoke for the North, nominated Abraham Lincoln. Lincoln opposed slavery's extension and hoped to keep the country from splitting up over the slavery question.

The just-formed Constitutional Union Party nominated John Bell of Tennessee. The Constitutional Unionists spoke for preserving the Union but remained silent on the question of slavery.

The Democrats wrangled over their platform until southern delegates walked out of the convention. Those who remained named Senator Stephen Douglas, who spoke for popular sovereignty. Settlers, not Congress, he said, would decide for themselves the issue of extending slavery into their territories.

Southern Democrats named a candidate of their own, Vice President John Breckinridge. For them, the issue was extending slavery into the new territories, not preserving the Union.

During the race, party supporters handed out biographies and pamphlets and spoke on behalf of the nominees. Photographs of all four men flooded the market, the first use of photography in presidential politics. But three of the candidates—Bell, Breckinridge, and Lincoln—endorsed the tradition of the noncampaign.

A campaign button for Abraham Lincoln reads, "The Great Rail-Splitter of the West Must & Shall Be Our Next President." Pioneers split logs to make their fence rails, so this nickname linked Lincoln with his days as a settler of Illinois.

Four parties and their candidates vied for the presidency in the 1860 election. In this political cartoon from 1860, Republican Abraham Lincoln (left) *and Democrat Stephen Douglas* (second from left) *argue over the western territories on a map of the United States. Southern Democrat John Breckinridge* (second from right) *tries to separate the South, and Constitutional Unionist John Bell* (right) *tries to tape the Union back together.*

Abraham Lincoln waited at his home in Springfield, Illinois, and welcomed party leaders, friends, and even reporters. But he did not speak on politics or issues. When asked where he stood, he replied, "Those who will not read or heed what I have already publicly said, would not read or heed a repetition of it."

Lincoln's fellow Republicans took up his slack. Carrying torchlights, a group of mostly young men, called Wide Awakes, dazzled the voters with their military-style marches. Wearing glazed capes and caps to keep dripping oil from their torches from ruining their clothing, they paraded through cities, often in a zigzag pattern, singing songs and chanting slogans.

Only Stephen Douglas dared to defy tradition. Douglas offered Americans a first-ever national stumping tour. Candidates in state and local elections would often address gathered crowds while standing on a tree stump. This electioneering was called "on the stump." Douglas campaigned by traveling from place to place giving political speeches to the gathered throngs. He didn't announce he would take to the stump, though. Instead, he explained his journeys as a visit to his mother who lived in upstate New York.

By campaign's end, he'd crossed the country and delivered countless speeches, sometimes twenty a day. He preached his slogan, "The Union Now and Forever" and begged for the compromise of popular sovereignty, allowing territorial settlers to decide the slavery issue themselves. Douglas addressed the citizens of Raleigh, North Carolina, on August 30, 1860, on this topic. ". . . having so deep a stake in the Union, we are determined to maintain it and we know but one mode by which it can be maintained; that is to enforce rigidly . . . the Constitution." The Constitution allowed for local self-government, and Douglas believed the settlers themselves should choose what they wanted to do about legalizing slavery in their state.

Despite the seriousness of his message, his enemies ridiculed him— for stumping. His critics mocked him as the lost son, since it had taken weeks to reach his mother. As for his words of compromise, hecklers threw eggs and rotten fruit at him, even threatened his life.

Lincoln won the election and became the first-ever Republican president. Except for New Jersey, a united North gave him 180 electoral votes but only 40 percent of the popular vote. Breckinridge took most of the slave states (72 electoral votes, 18 percent of the popular vote), followed by John Bell (39 and 13 percent). Stephen Douglas trailed with 12 electoral votes and 29.5 percent of the popular vote. After his win, Lincoln told the press, "Well, boys, your troubles are over, mine have just begun."

With the election final, the southern states worried that Lincoln would abolish slavery. South Carolina, Florida, Mississippi, Georgia, Louisiana, Alabama, and Texas seceded from the Union and formed the Confederate States of America. On April 12, 1861, South Carolina fired on the federally held Fort Sumter and started the U.S. Civil War. Virginia, North Carolina, Arkansas, and Tennessee joined the Confederacy.

Even at war, the Union held elections in 1864. Republicans, now called the National Unity Party to lure more voters, renominated Lincoln along with pro-war Democrat, Andrew Johnson of Tennessee, for the vice presidency. Democrats went with former U.S. Army commander George McClellan, who had been fired by Lincoln for inaction in battle. In this race, neither man campaigned.

War, of course, was the issue. However, for Lincoln, so was the abolition of slavery. In 1863 he issued the Emancipation Proclamation, which freed slaves in the Confederate states. But he pressed for an end to slavery everywhere in the United States.

GRAND NATIONAL DEMOCRATIC BANNER.
PEACE! UNION! AND VICTORY!

"Peace! Union! and Victory!" declares an 1864 campaign banner for George B. McClellan and his running mate, George H. Pendleton. The hands clasped below the portraits are a signal of peace and union. The busy harbor scene shows prosperity—the results of peace and union.

In the Democratic camp, those who wanted to end the fighting and negotiate peace were called "Copperheads," named for a kind of poisonous snake. Candidate McClellan broke with his party and insisted on a final victory.

"It seems exceedingly probable that this administration will not be reelected," Lincoln wrote early in 1864, for the war was going badly. By September, however, Union general William Sherman had marched on Atlanta, Georgia, and other Union victories followed. The voters handed the president a second term. Accepting his nomination in 1864, he wrote, "I approve the declaration in favor of so amending the Constitution as to prohibit Slavery throughout the nation." In 1865 Congress passed the Thirteenth Amendment, which ended slavery.

On April 9, 1865, Confederate general Robert E. Lee surrendered to Union general Ulysses S. Grant. On April 14, a southern sympathizer, John Wilkes Booth, fired at Lincoln while he watched a play at Ford's Theatre in Washington, D.C. Nine hours later, Lincoln lay dead, the country's first assassinated president.

During his time in office, Abraham Lincoln altered the American way of life. In his own way, Stephen Douglas's campaign also caused significant changes. Future candidates would look to his historic race as they plotted their own stumping strategies.

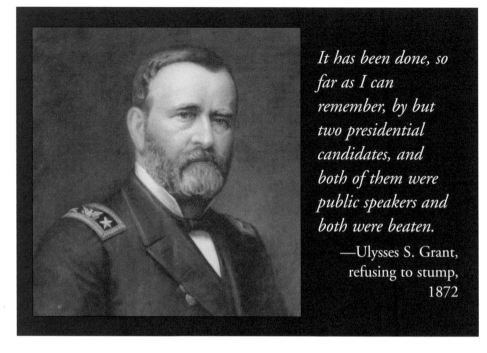

It has been done, so far as I can remember, by but two presidential candidates, and both of them were public speakers and both were beaten.

—Ulysses S. Grant, refusing to stump, 1872

WINDS OF CHANGE

WITH NO DUE RESPECT

The contests following the Civil War focused on the serious issue of Reconstruction (1865–1877)—a system of rebuilding the South, reorganizing its governments, and determining how the defeated states would rejoin the Union. Many congressional Republicans, the Radicals, demanded harsh restrictions for the former Confederacy. They called for suffrage (voting rights) for black freedmen of the South, even though, at this time, northern states were allowed to decide for themselves whether black males would vote.

In 1868 Republicans nominated the commander of the Union forces,

Ulysses S. Grant, as their candidate for president. "Let us have peace," Grant wrote in his letter of acceptance. At that time, a candidate formally acknowledged his letter of nomination with a letter of acceptance.

Democrats compromised on Horatio Seymour, governor of New York. Their platform considered Reconstruction "unconstitutional, revolutionary, and void."

During the race, Grant bowed to the still-accepted tradition of staying home and refusing to discuss issues. For a while, Seymour also minded presidential candidate manners. Only when his defeat seemed certain did he brave public opinion. He visited a handful of cities in New York, Pennsylvania, Ohio, Indiana, and Illinois. Still, Seymour lost to Grant. The black freedmen, who voted for the first time ever, helped Grant edge out a narrow win of popular votes.

Grant took office in March 1869, and shortly after that, Congress passed the Fifteenth Amendment, making it illegal to deny voting rights "on account of race, color, or previous condition of servitude."

Black freedmen voted for the first time in U.S. history in Washington, D.C., on June 3, 1867. This illustration was published in Harper's Weekly *in June 1867.*

Still, groups of hate-filled men formed the Ku Klux Klan, an organization that terrorized and murdered former slaves. In spite of this, Mississippian Hiram Revels became the country's first black senator. The Mississippi legislature voted him into office when a vacancy occurred. At that time, state legislatures still appointed senators.

In 1872 the president's supporters clamored for a second Grant term. But liberals in the Republican Party, disgusted with both Reconstruction and the scandals and corruption that tainted Grant's administration, denounced him. Instead, they turned to Horace Greeley, editor of the *New York Tribune* and a founder of their party. In an unusual twist of politics, given that Greeley had often blasted them in his newspaper, Democrats nominated him as well.

Once again, Grant sat out the race. He said of campaigning, "It has been done, so far as I remember, by but two presidential candidates, and both of them were public speakers and both were beaten."

Born free in 1822 in North Carolina, Hiram Revels (left) *settled in Natchez, Mississippi, and became the first African American to serve in the U.S. Senate (1870–1871). In 1875 a second black senator, Blanche K. Bruce, also from Mississippi, would be elected to the Senate. But nearly a century passed before another African American would be elected again—Edward Brooke of Massachussets, who was elected in 1967.*

Greeley, however, swung through several key states and offered over two hundred speeches. Even in 1872, though, critics mocked him for appealing directly to the public. Greeley, sick and saddened by the death of his wife during the campaign, died a month after the election, before the Electoral College met. Most of his sixty-six electoral votes were eventually dispersed among other would-be presidential candidates. Despite his death, three Electoral College members still voted for Greeley. The voters, however, returned Grant to the White House.

Although Grant and Greeley dominated the campaign news in 1872, a woman also grabbed the nation's attention. In New York, Susan B. Anthony broke the national law and voted. Police arrested her, and the courts tried her, found her guilty, and fined her. Anthony refused to pay a cent of that fine.

In 1876, as the election approached, the United States celebrated its one hundredth birthday. The typewriter and the telephone had been invented. Baseball's National League began to play ball. In South Dakota, the tribes of the Cheyenne and Sioux decimated General George Custer and his troops in the Battle of the Little Bighorn. During Grant's second term, the United States experienced a financial depression.

Although the Civil War had been over for eleven years, the Republicans "waved the bloody shirt" during the campaign. They blamed the South for starting the war and reminded voters of the soldiers' sacrifices. Their candidate, Rutherford B. Hayes, Ohio's governor, said of the tactic, "It leads people away from hard times, which is our deadliest foe."

Hayes considered other issues too. Bothered by Grant's scandal-ridden administration, Hayes supported civil service reform. Up until this time, election winners in state, local, and national races had the right to appoint their supporters to government positions, whether they were qualified or not. Many wanted an end to this system called patronage. Hayes's Democratic opponent, Governor Samuel Tilden of New York, also called for reform.

In 1876 neither candidate actively campaigned. Hayes laid out his agenda in his acceptance letter but mostly said nothing about his positions. "Silence is the only safety," he remarked. Democrats offered the voters a "campaign textbook," which included information about Tilden, party platforms, and an account of Grant's messy government. Both parties organized torchlight parades and songfests and spoke out for the candidates.

As the race neared its end, Hayes worried about a loss. With the count finished on November 8, Tilden led with 51 percent of the popular vote and 184 electoral votes, one vote away from a win.

In Louisiana, South Carolina, and Florida, however, no one knew just who had won. Republicans and Democrats both insisted their man had been victorious, and each charged the other with voting fraud. In Oregon, officials questioned one of their electoral votes. The twenty votes that hung in the balance could give Hayes the presidency.

The Constitution offered no resolution, so Congress chose a fifteen-member commission to untangle the mess. The eight

This cartoon appeared in a New York City newspaper in January 1877, while the results of the 1876 election were still undecided. It shows a U.S. soldier thrusting the contested election returns from South Carolina, Louisiana, and Florida at Rutherford B. Hayes.

Republicans and seven Democrats gave the disputed votes to Hayes. Although Tilden took the popular vote (51 percent to 48 percent), "Rutherfraud," as his opponents called him, had the electoral margin, 185 to 184. Of his loss, Tilden said, "I can retire to private life with the consciousness that I shall receive from posterity the credit of having been elected to the highest position in the gift of the people without any of the cares and responsibilities of the office."

Some Democrats threatened to prevent Congress from officially approving the commission's decision. Voters worried that the chaos would result in another civil war. But Republican and Democratic leaders finally negotiated a deal. In the Compromise of 1877, Republicans agreed to end Reconstruction by removing all remaining troops in the South, thus leaving the Democrats in charge of their state and local governments. In return, Democrats promised to guarantee African Americans their rights and to accept the Republican as president. On March 2, 1877, two days before the scheduled inauguration, Congress approved the Hayes presidency.

Shortly after he took office, Hayes withdrew all government troops from the South. Democrats in power there, however, prevented African Americans from voting and refused to uphold their constitutional rights. African Americans would wait almost another century before these bars would be lifted.

ONCE UPON A PORCH

President Hayes decided against a second term in 1880, so Republicans chose longtime congressman James Garfield of Ohio, with Chester A. Arthur as his running mate. Democrats named Winfield Scott Hancock of Pennsylvania, a Union army general, who had no political record or experience.

One issue in the contest was the tariff, which is a tax on imported goods. Republicans called for a high tariff. This would protect American products from having to compete with less expensive ones coming in from overseas. Hancock dismissed the tariff as a local question and drew criticism for his remarks. Only the U.S. government can impose tariffs, so it was more than a local concern.

Another issue in the contest was Chinese immigration. Especially in the West, Chinese immigrants could be hired for cheaper wages than white Americans and were accused of taking jobs from American citizens. Both candidates called for restrictions on such immigration.

Both parties still talked about civil service reform. Hoping to appeal to all factions of Republicans, Garfield vaguely endorsed a program of reforms. Hancock favored them too.

The Greenback Labor Party's James Weaver called for an eight-hour workday, women's suffrage, and protection of black voting rights.

True to tradition, Hancock stayed out of the contest, avoided the issues, and let others speak for him. James Garfield, however, took command of his race. He not only planned strategy, but using a new campaign technique, he welcomed visitors who streamed to his home in Mentor, Ohio, hoping to catch a glimpse of a presidential candidate. Small groups and large ones, children and adults, men and

In 1880 James Weaver ran for president on the Greenback Labor Party ticket. The Greenback Party was so named because it favored a paper money (greenbacks) over metal coins. The party also supported financial assistance to farmers, an income tax, an eight-hour workday, and women's suffrage.

women, politicians, and everyday citizens all came to look over Garfield and hear him speak. They waved flags and banners, sang songs, and tramped on the grass. Garfield greeted his guests from his front porch and spoke to them. His wife offered them cold drinks.

While Garfield addressed the throngs, fellow Republicans published "A Record of the Statesmanship and Political Achievements of General Winfield Scott Hancock"—eight blank pages.

With the vote counted, Garfield squeaked to victory, 48.5 percent to 48.1 percent, 214 electoral votes to 155. On his defeat, Hancock said, "That is all right. I can stand it." The Greenback Labor Party's Weaver received 300,000 votes.

On July 2, 1881, a disgruntled and mentally unbalanced office seeker, Charles Guiteau, fired a gun at Garfield in a Washington, D.C., train station. Doctors couldn't find the bullet, and Garfield clung to life for more than two months. He finally died on September 19. Vice President Chester Arthur completed Garfield's term.

In the 1884 contest, the Republican convention named James G. Blaine as the party's candidate. With his nomination, a group of convention delegates called mugwumps (from a Native American Algonquin word meaning "big chief") walked out. They favored civil service reform, while Blaine did not.

The Democrats nominated Grover Cleveland, known as Uncle Jumbo to his relatives. (He weighed over 250 pounds.) Neither Blaine nor Cleveland conducted a front porch campaign. Cleveland made only two appearances, while Blaine stumped for about six weeks and gave about four hundred short speeches. Cleveland won and became the first Democrat to occupy the White House in twenty-four years.

During his term, with the coming of railroads, the United States divided into time zones. Until then every area used the sun to set its own time. But the railroads, needing exact schedules, helped establish standard time zones for the country. In 1886 the president dedicated the Statue of Liberty, and Coca-Cola went on sale in Atlanta, Georgia.

By 1888 Cleveland decided to run again. The Beast of Buffalo, as

Cleveland was sometimes called because of his size, would battle Benjamin Harrison, former senator from Indiana, often referred to as the Human Iceberg because of his aloof personality.

As a sitting president, Cleveland followed the long-standing tradition and did not campaign. Harrison didn't stump either. "I have a great risk of meeting a fool at home," he said, "but the candidate who travels cannot escape him." Instead, he conducted his own front porch campaign, offering greetings and comments on the need for a high protective tariff, a major issue, in over eighty speeches to three hundred thousand visitors. Cleveland called for a reduced tariff.

Log cabins, huge rolling balls, banners, and brass bands also lured the crowds in 1888 for Harrison was the grandson of Old Tippecanoe, ninth president, William Henry Harrison. Republicans even chanted the old slogan with a new twist, "Tippecanoe and Morton Too." Levi P. Morton was the vice-presidential candidate.

Benjamin Harrison's campaign raised huge amounts of money, much of which came from big business. Some of these funds helped to pay for voting scams. For instance, local political promoters sometimes paid for votes. Indiana did not require its citizens to register in order to cast

This large ball was part of Benjamin Harrison's front porch campaign. Supporters rolled the ball, on which various slogans had been written, from town to town to drum up voter support for the new Tippecanoe.

a ballot, so the promoters paid for repeaters, people who voted more than once. In Indiana, especially, where a win was crucial, repeaters could change their names, disguise themselves, and vote again. (Since colored ballots identifying party preference were used at that time, politicians could tell if a repeater had earned his pay.) After this election, several states amended their laws, and by 1892, more than thirty states would require a secret ballot to protect a voter's privacy.

Benjamin Harrison swept the electoral vote, 233 to 168, and took the presidency even though he lost the popular vote, 48 percent to 49 percent. This was the third time this had happened.

In 1892 the contest featured a rematch between Harrison and Cleveland, arguing over the tariff as they had four years earlier. A third party, the People's, or Populist, Party, ran James Weaver. Weaver spoke on behalf of the rural and urban working poor. He demanded federal ownership of railroads, telegraphs, and telephones, a graduated income tax, and direct election of U.S. senators. Weaver also called for unlimited minting of silver coins to increase the supply of money. This extra money would make it easier for debtors to pay off what they owed. Populists crossed the country and preached their cause.

Benjamin Harrison didn't campaign because he was worried about his wife who was ill with tuberculosis. Caroline Harrison died two weeks before the election.

Grover Cleveland began his campaign by breaking tradition (and appalling Republicans). Instead of the usual letter of acceptance, Cleveland spoke before a throng of thousands at the Democratic convention in Madison Square Garden in New York and formally accepted his nomination. Without microphones, however, the noisy crowd could hardly hear him.

Cleveland won and became the only candidate to serve nonconsecutive terms. The Populists carried four states and received twenty-two electoral votes. Harrison, mourning his wife, said, "For me there is no sting in defeat. Indeed after the heavy blow the death of my wife dealt me, I do not think I could have stood the strain a reelection would have brought."

A national campaign for the presidency is to me a nightmare.
—William H. Taft, 1908

ON THE FRONT LINES

THE BATTLE OF THE BUGS

During Cleveland's second term, many railroads, banks, and other commercial businesses failed and caused a financial panic. The depression that followed led to large-scale unemployment. Because of this dire situation, the 1896 election focused on economics.

Some people believed that the country should go to a gold standard. This would mean that ordinary paper money could be cashed in for gold kept in reserve in the federal mint. Others, especially farmers and silver miners, demanded free and unlimited coinage of silver dollars to pay off their debts. More silver dollars would also enable consumers to buy more. Those favoring silver pushed for a ratio of 16 to 1—sixteen ounces of silver would be equal to one ounce of gold.

The Republican convention settled on the gold standard and nominated Ohio governor William McKinley. Republicans who supported a silver standard walked out of the party convention. Eventually, they supported the Democratic pro-silver candidate.

At the still-undecided Democratic convention, Nebraska delegate William Jennings Bryan addressed the crowd and called for the coinage of silver. "[W]e will answer their demand for a gold standard," Bryan exclaimed, "by saying to them: you shall not press down upon the brow of labor this crown of thorns, you shall not crucify mankind upon a cross of gold."

Afterward, the thirty-six-year-old Bryan confided to his wife, "I am the only man who can be nominated. I am what they call 'the logic of the situation.'" The convention agreed he was the logical choice and named him as their candidate. Gold standard Democrats left their convention when it adopted a silver platform. They formed a party of their own, the National Democratic Party, and ran John M. Palmer as their candidate.

Despite the party's gold stand, McKinley waffled over the money controversy, preferring to talk tariffs instead. A high tariff, he explained, would mean less competition from abroad for American industries, and it would encourage greater employment and better salaries for workers. McKinley promised Americans a "Full Dinner Pail"—jobs, financial security, and all-around prosperity. Bryan wouldn't let the gold-silver issue die, though. "Sixteen to One," his supporters chanted until McKinley finally came out for the gold standard.

During the campaign, Bryan took to the stump and crossed the country in an unheard-of whistle-stop tour. Trains signaled short stops in small towns with a whistle toot. Shouting from the back platform of his train without a microphone, he gave twenty, sometimes more, speeches a day. By the time the competition was over,

William Jennings Bryan speaks to a crowd from a railroad car during his whistle-stop campaign tour of 1896.

Bryan had covered eighteen thousand miles, traveled through twenty-seven states, and used his powerful voice to sway voters.

Republican William McKinley never left his home in Canton, Ohio. "I might just as well put up a trapeze on my front lawn and compete with some professional athlete as go out speaking against Bryan," he said. Instead, 750,000 Americans came to him. At home, decked out with a red carnation, McKinley addressed his visitors. He reviewed beforehand the topics his guests planned to introduce and then carefully prepared his remarks.

Those who couldn't go to see the candidate learned about him through pamphlets, posters, and leaflets. The Republicans also sent out over a thousand speakers, who roamed the United States promoting McKinley.

Americans enthusiastically took sides in the contest. Gold folk—easterners, businessmen, and industrialists—displayed gold bug pins on their lapels. Silverites—westerners and poor, small-farm owners—wore silver bugs. For the first time, voters sported campaign buttons with attached pins on the back.

With all forty-five states in the Union voting, McKinley took the win. During his term, he and Congress pushed through a high protective tariff, the Dingley Tariff, and the Gold Standard Act. Prosperity returned. American dinner pails were full.

During McKinley's first term, Cuba, at that time a colony of Spain, demanded its independence. Although the U.S. president took no official stand, the government sent the battleship *Maine* into the Havana harbor as a show of support for Cuba. On February 15, 1898, the *Maine* exploded, killing more than 260 sailors.

"Remember the *Maine*," newspaper headlines and the public screamed, blaming Spain for the explosion. Goaded by the newspaper and public opinion, McKinley asked Congress to declare war on Spain.

After the four-month Spanish-American War in Cuba, the United States defeated Spain. Cuba was freed, but with the peace terms, the United States acquired Puerto Rico and the Spanish possessions of Guam and the Philippines in the Pacific Ocean. The United States had become an imperial power, controlling the political and economic affairs of countries beyond its borders.

Republicans renominated McKinley in 1900 along with New York governor Theodore Roosevelt as the vice-presidential candidate. McKinley ran a quiet race. He considered it undignified for a president to campaign. Roosevelt and the Democratic candidate, William Jennings Bryan, did hit the trail. Bryan raged against U.S. imperialism.

McKinley earned an easy victory, 292 electoral votes to 155. Voter participation registered 73 percent, the last time the turnout in an election was over 70 percent.

Six months into McKinley's second term, an anarchist, Leon Czolgosz, shot him. (An anarchist is a person who rebels against the authority of a government.) Eight days later, on September 14, 1901, McKinley died in office. The Secret Service, formed in 1865 to clamp down on counterfeiting, took over the job of protecting the president after this assassination.

Theodore Roosevelt finished out McKinley's term. In 1904 Roosevelt ran for the office in his own right against Democrat Alton B. Parker, a New York judge, and won. He became the first "accidental president" (one who replaces a president who died in office) to get a term of his own. Until then, other vice presidents who became president upon the death of the chief—John Tyler, Millard Fillmore, Andrew Johnson, and Chester Arthur—were never elected to their own terms.

Roosevelt did not run again in 1908. Instead, Republicans named his preferred successor, William Taft, as the party candidate. Taft faced Democratic challenger William Jennings Bryan, running for a third time.

While Bryan took to the stump, Taft, at first, preferred the golf course to campaigning. "A national campaign for the presidency is to me a nightmare," he said. However, he eventually bowed to Roosevelt's pressure, hit the campaign trail, and won. For the first time ever, two presidential candidates stumped the United States looking for votes.

William Howard Taft preferred playing golf to campaigning. Here he is shown on the golf course in Hot Springs, Virginia, in 1908.

This political cartoon shows Theodore Roosevelt's shock at the way President Taft (left) had overseen the policies (represented here by a scrawny cat) that Roosevelt (right) had put in place during his first term as president. In an unprecedented move, a former two-term president ran for a third, nonconsecutive term after leaving the presidency.

A WHOLE LOT OF STUMPING GOING ON

In 1912 Theodore Roosevelt, demanding reforms for a better America, challenged President Taft for the Republican nomination. "My hat is in the ring," he proclaimed.

In 1912 voters in twelve states participated in primary elections for the first time, after cries for reform and a more democratic nominating process. The primary voters either chose the delegates to the national convention, voted for their preference for their party's nominee, or both. Up until then, powerful party bosses often dictated who the delegates should be and who they should nominate.

Roosevelt and Taft stumped the country, seeking primary wins and attacking each other. "Fathead," Roosevelt called his former friend, who weighed over three hundred pounds. "Dangerous egotist," Taft retorted.

Taft was the first sitting president to appeal directly to the voting public. Later, after the Republican convention, Taft would say, "Precedents of propriety were broken in a President's taking the stump, much to the pain and discomfit of many . . . citizens . . . but the course thus taken was necessary to avert a National calamity [Roosevelt's nomination]."

When the Republicans finally met in Chicago, Illinois, in June, Roosevelt had the majority of primary wins. Party bosses, however, awarded Taft some contested delegates, so he received the nomination. Roosevelt supporters left the gathering, formed their own Progressive Party, and nominated Teddy. When he announced, "I'm feeling like a bull moose," they nicknamed themselves the Bull Moose Party.

In late June, Democrats chose their nominee, New Jersey governor Woodrow Wilson. Wilson set the tone for his race in his acceptance speech. "A presidential campaign may easily degenerate into a mere personal contest and so lose its real dignity and significance. There is no indispensable man."

President Taft said early in the race, "I think I might as well give up so far as being a candidate is concerned. There are so many people in the country who don't like me."

While Taft didn't stump, Roosevelt and Wilson stormed into the campaign, running as reformers. Roosevelt promised "A Square Deal All Around" and flaunted his New Nationalism, which included government regulation of big business corporations. Many prosperous businesses had merged to become large enough to stifle competition. They were called trusts. He also promised tariff revision, women's suffrage, and an end to child labor. Wilson preached his New Freedom reforms. Unlike Roosevelt, who wanted to regulate trusts, Wilson would break them up and open competition.

On October 14, would-be assassin John Shrank fired a shot at Roosevelt and wounded him in the chest. Roosevelt insisted on completing his speech before seeking medical treatment. His opponents rested their races while he recovered.

On Election Day, Republicans split their votes between Roosevelt and Taft. Wilson took 435 electoral votes and 42 percent of the popular vote, Roosevelt, 88 electoral votes and 27 percent, and Taft trailed behind with 8 votes and 23 percent. Woodrow Wilson was the first candidate to be elected president by actively campaigning.

Wilson worked on domestic reform issues. He pushed the Federal Reserve Act through Congress. The act created a national banking system and the Federal Trade Commission, a watchdog organization that regulated business practices. When World War I (1914–1918), the Great War, began in Europe in August 1914, Wilson promised American neutrality.

In 1916 Wilson sought the presidency again, running on the slogan, "He Kept Us Out of War." During the campaign, Wilson addressed crowds from his home for the most part, but he made some speeches on the campaign trail. He stood behind his record of reform. Ribbons, campaign buttons, posters, pennants, and speeches presented in movie theater newsreels (a new film innovation) helped spread his message.

Wilson was opposed by Republican Charles Evans Hughes, a Supreme Court justice. Hughes stumped the country, accompanied by Antoinette Hughes, a first such tour for a candidate's wife.

By nightfall of election day, Hughes believed he had won. So did Wilson! Two days later, with California's vote final, Wilson clinched the victory. One month after his inauguration, Woodrow Wilson asked Congress for a declaration of war. German submarines had been attacking U.S. ships sailing the Atlantic, causing damage and costing lives. Siding with the Allies, which included Great Britain, France, Russia, and Italy, Wilson said, "The world must be made safe for democracy."

The United States and the Allies won World War I with a truce declared on November 11, 1918. The peace treaty ending the war called for a League of Nations, an organization of countries working to ensure world peace. The U.S. Congress refused to ratify the treaty, so Wilson traveled the country, appealing directly to the public. On September 25, 1919, an ailing president returned to the White

Carrie Chapman Catt (center), *a leader of the women's suffrage movement, stands in line with other women to cast her ballot in the 1920 election—the first U.S. election open to women voters.*

House, where he suffered a paralyzing stroke. In an unusual turn of events, his wife Edith secretly handled his affairs, and together they watched Wilson's vision die.

Republican Warren Harding demanded a "Return to Normalcy" in the 1920 contest. (He misstated the word *normality.*) He and many others yearned for what seemed like a simpler life before war. Even his campaign glorified the past, as he mostly met Americans from his front porch in Marion, Ohio. His Democratic opponent, James Cox, on the other hand, traveled the country, along with his running mate, Franklin Delano Roosevelt.

That 1920 race included two never-befores. With the passage of the Nineteenth Amendment in 1920, women were finally allowed to vote. And in Pittsburgh, Pennsylvania, for the first time ever, a radio station, KDKA, broadcast election results: 404 electoral votes for Harding to 127 for Cox. A minor party candidate, Socialist Eugene Debs, ran his campaign from a prison cell. He'd been jailed for speaking out against World War I.

Harding died midterm in 1923 amidst a scandal-ridden adminis-tration. One of the best known of them was the Teapot Dome scan-dal. Secretary of the Interior Albert B. Fall had taken a bribe in exchange for allowing private companies to lease government oil reserves. Upon Harding's death, Vice President Calvin Coolidge took the oath of office and then ran for the presidency in 1924.

In 1924 the Progressive Party candidate, Robert LaFollette of Wis-consin, and Coolidge's Democratic opponent, John W. Davis of West Virginia, both stumped around the country. The Democratic conven-tion had been deadlocked for an unheard of 103 ballots until it finally compromised on Davis. Calvin Coolidge did not stump. It may have been because his sixteen-year-old son had died from blood poisoning shortly after the convention. Voter turnout was low, but Coolidge won with 382 electoral votes to 136 for Davis and 13 for LaFollette. Coolidge won his race without crisscrossing the country. But by the beginning of the next decade, stumping would become an accepted, even expected way of political life.

EUGENE VICTOR DEBS

A campaign postcard for Eugene Victor Debs pictures him in the Atlanta, Georgia, prison. Debs was arrested in 1918 under the Espionage (spying) Act of 1917 for making an antiwar speech protesting the United States' entrance into World War I. He was serving out his ten-year prison sentence when he campaigned for U.S. president on the Socialist Party ticket. Debs had also run for president in 1904, 1908, and 1912.

Growth and development of the use of the radio was such that in 1928 it played probably the most important role in the national campaign.

—Al Smith, in his 1929 autobiography

Al Smith on the campaign trail with two donkeys—symbols of the Democratic Party

TECHNOLOGICAL WONDERS

STAY TUNED

By the 1920s, radio had taken its own place in politics. In 1924 it aired the conventions. By 1928 Americans listened together, one united audience, as the candidates addressed them in radio speeches at the convention and on the campaign trail.

Calvin Coolidge had declined a second term, so Herbert Hoover of California represented the Republicans. New York governor Al Smith was the Democratic candidate. Smith was the first Roman Catholic ever to receive a presidential nomination.

During the campaign, Herbert Hoover emphasized that eight years of Republican policies had fired up the economy. In his nomination acceptance speech, August 1928, he'd stressed to the gathered crowd and to the equally important radio listeners, "We in America today are nearer to the final triumph over poverty than ever before in the history of any land. The poorhouse is vanishing from among us."

Other issues, besides the economy, mattered in this contest. Hoover favored Prohibition, the Eighteenth Amendment (1920) to the Constitution, which outlawed alcoholic beverages in the United States. They couldn't be made, sold, or even transported. Alcohol could still be used as medicine or for religious observance, however. Al Smith did not favor Prohibition.

Many voters supported the Eighteenth Amendment and refused to consider a Smith presidency. Some claimed his New York accent

Herbert Hoover broadcast his final campaign speech before the election on November 5, 1928. Radio changed the way national campaigns were run, as candidates could share their message with listeners across the United States. As radio broadcasts reached more Americans, including less educated and less politically active populations, more voters turned up at the polls.

grated on their ears. Many others worried about his religion. Americans wondered if he'd be loyal to the pope (the leader of the Catholic Church) or the flag.

Smith confronted the issue of his Catholicism. On September 20, he said, "The constitutional guaranty that there should be no religious test for public office is not a mere form of words. I attack those who seek to undermine it. The absolute separation of state and church is part of the fundamental basis of our Constitution."

Hoover didn't attack the governor's religious beliefs, but he rarely tried to stop others from spouting insults. He didn't debate or discuss other public concerns either. During his campaign, he made only seven major speeches, all of them broadcast on the radio.

Hoover wrote about his radio experiences in his memoirs. "That invention," he said, "had made it impossible for Presidential candidates to repeat the same speech with small variations, as had been the practice in those happier speaking times."

In his autobiography, Smith acknowledged, "Growth and development of the use of the radio was such that in 1928 it played probably the most important role in the national campaign."

Hoover won in a landslide victory, 444 electoral votes to 87 for Smith, and in his inaugural address, he said of the future, "It is bright with hope." Seven months later, in October 1929, the stock market crashed. Millions of people lost everything. The United States spiraled into the worst economic crisis in its history, the Great Depression (1929–1942).

In 1932 the president's campaign slogan, "Prosperity is near," gave little hope to Americans who waited in breadlines for food, sold apples for a nickel, and lived in shantytowns nicknamed Hoovervilles. Still, when the Republicans gathered in Chicago for their 1932 convention, they again turned to Herbert Hoover.

The Democrats settled on New York governor Franklin Delano Roosevelt. The public didn't know that Roosevelt wore steel braces on his legs because polio had paralyzed them. Roosevelt promised a different way of handling the financial crisis.

Franklin Delano Roosevelt (**right**) *campaigned for president in 1932. He was paralyzed from the waist down after contracting polio in 1921. In order not to appear weak and sickly in public, Roosevelt's legs were fitted with braces so that he could walk short distances. He is shown here on the campaign trail—standing but supported by an open car door.*

Unlike other candidates, Roosevelt went to the convention in person and addressed the crowd as well as the radio audience. "The appearance before a National Convention of its nominee for President," he said, "to be formally notified of his selection, is unprecedented and unusual, but these are unprecedented and unusual times. I have started out on the tasks that lie ahead by breaking the absurd traditions that the candidate should remain in professed ignorance of what has happened for weeks until he is formally notified of that event. You have nominated me and I know it, and I am here to thank you for the honor." Roosevelt concluded with these words, "I pledge you, I pledge myself to a new deal for the American people."

Roosevelt barreled through America in his six-car special train, blasting Hoover and radiating confidence. By autumn Hoover realized that he must get out and take his message to the people. His speeches—he was the last president to write them himself—drew boos. People chanted, "In Hoover We Trusted: Now We Are Busted." Like Roosevelt, he also took to the radio.

That November Roosevelt crushed Hoover with 472 electoral votes to 59. Just before his inauguration, Roosevelt was the victim of an attempted assassination. Guiseppe Zangara, an out-of-work bricklayer, missed the president-elect but killed Chicago's mayor, who was with him.

The new president took office on March 4, 1933. The Twentieth Amendment moved inauguration day from March to January 20 in future elections. Within the first hundred days, Roosevelt pushed several bills through Congress to help fight the Depression. He also addressed Americans gathered around their radios in what he called fireside chats.

By 1936 some of the desperation of the Depression had eased. The Democrats renominated Roosevelt for a second term. At this convention for the first time, a candidate needed only a simple majority of votes to receive the Democratic nomination. Previously, a would-be candidate needed two-thirds of the delegates' votes. Roosevelt ran against Republican Alfred M. Landon, governor of Kansas.

In this race, both parties used preference polls, which queried prospective voters on their choice of candidate. Based on these polls, each side predicted its own win. The *Literary Digest* poll, which had

Alfred M. Landon is pictured here in 1936 with members of the Women's American Legion Auxiliary of Kansas.

Some Democrats who opposed Roosevelt's third bid for the presidency supported Republican Wendell Willkie. In this campaign poster, Uncle Sam gives a thumbs down for a third Roosevelt term. Roosevelt would go on to win a third and a fourth term!

correctly picked a winner since the 1920 election, forecast a win for Landon. The victory, though, went to Roosevelt, who scored the biggest electoral margin since 1820: 523 electoral votes to 8. Roosevelt took all states but Maine and Vermont.

In 1940 Roosevelt ran for an unprecedented third time against Republican Wendell Willkie and again won. During this term, Roosevelt focused on foreign affairs. Overseas, the German army, directed by the country's dictator, Adolf Hitler, had conquered much of Europe. On December 7, 1941, Japan, which sided with Germany, attacked the U.S. naval base at Pearl Harbor in Hawaii. The United States declared war on Japan and Germany and joined forces with the Allies—Britain (which Germany had not invaded) and the Soviet Union.

Despite World War II (1939–1945), the United States held elections in 1944. Roosevelt ran for a fourth term, against Republican Thomas E. Dewey and defeated him. He did not live to see the end of the war and an American victory, however. On April 12, 1945, Roosevelt died of a cerebral hemorrhage, massive bleeding in the brain. As radio reported the news, Americans mourned the death of this larger-than-life president.

ALL ABOARD

Harry Truman became America's seventh accidental president, the seventh vice president to take office. While he completed Roosevelt's term, the Allies declared victory in Europe on May 8, 1945. Truman made the decision to drop atomic bombs on two Japanese cities to hasten the end of the war. Japan surrendered on August 14, 1945.

Peace, however, didn't bring an end to Truman's problems. After the war, consumers wanted to buy items that had been scarce or rationed during the conflict, but suppliers couldn't produce them fast enough. Prices soared, and workers struck for higher wages so they could afford the higher cost of living. Americans blamed Truman for these economic woes, and his approval rating plummeted.

In 1947 the mostly Republican 80th Congress pushed for a Twenty-Second Amendment to the Constitution. Congress worried that future presidents elected to multiple terms, as Roosevelt had, could become too powerful. The amendment limited the president to

On April 13, 1945, newpapers from around the country, such as this one from the New York Herald Tribune, *bore headlines announcing Roosevelt's death and former vice president Harry Truman's succession to the presidency.*

just two terms in office. The amendment was finally ratified in 1951.

In 1948 Truman's friends advised him against running for his own term. But Truman threw his hat into the ring, saying, "I'm going to fight hard. I'm going to give them hell."

That year the Democrats splintered. Former New Dealers, who had supported the Roosevelt agenda, liberals, and American Communists formed a Progressive Party and named a former vice president, Henry Wallace, as their candidate. The Progressives wanted peace with the repressive Communist government of the Soviet Union. The Soviet Union and the United States were locked in the Cold War (1945–1991). This conflict was a battle involving differing forms of government and the struggle over influence around the world rather than actual fighting. The threat of war always hovered in the background, however. The Soviets had already extended their control over Eastern Europe. The United States wanted to prevent further Soviet influence in other parts of the world.

On the home front, segregationists disliked the strong civil rights stand in the Democratic Party platform. Among other items, the platform wanted to guarantee for all people, regardless of race, "the right to full and equal political participation; the right to equal opportunity of employment; the right of security of person; and the right of equal treatment in the service and defense of our nation." They left the Democratic Party and created the States' Rights Democrats (Dixiecrats) and chose South Carolina governor Strom Thurmond as their candidate.

The regular Democratic convention unenthusiastically nominated Harry Truman. Truman, however, believed he could win. In his acceptance speech, he blamed the 80th Congress, mostly Republican, for America's ills. This Congress had refused to enact programs Truman had proposed, legislation he felt would help Americans. He had called for additional public housing, legislation to help farmers, expansion of Social Security (which provided income for the elderly), and raising the minimum wage, all part of what he called his Fair Deal.

Truman stunned convention delegates and his radio audience by calling the legislators back for a special session of Congress after they had adjourned for the campaign season. This "do-nothing" Congress would have a chance to pass the programs Republicans also claimed to support. Delegates cheered for the feisty president who would take on Congress.

Truman's major rival was the Republican governor of New York, Thomas E. Dewey. Dewey had run against Franklin Roosevelt in 1944 and had put up a good fight. Despite Democratic taunts of "Phooey on Dewey," his supporters smelled a winner. "To Err is Truman," Republicans reminded the voters.

Aboard his railroad car, the *Ferdinand Magellan*, Harry Truman took to the tracks. In an unparalleled campaign, the last of its kind, the president whistle-stopped his way through thirty thousand miles of the United States. From the back platform of his train, Truman introduced his wife, Bess (the Boss), and presented his twenty-four-year-old daughter, Margaret (the Boss's Boss). Then he discussed his Fair Deal. He lashed out at the do-nothing Republican Congress again and again.

Aboard his *Victory Special*, Thomas Dewey didn't campaign nearly as hard since the opinion polls and newspapers had forecast his landslide win. Dewey refused to face Truman in debates and preferred not to discuss issues. Instead, he talked about American unity and seemed to echo Truman's platform.

Of his rival, the president said, "The Republican candidate is trying to run on the record of the Democratic Party. . . . He's a 'me too' man. Every time the Republican candidate looks at the program of the Democratic Party, he says, 'me too,' and his party's record says 'Nothing doing.'"

On election day, newspapers prepared their page-one stories. "Dewey Defeats Truman," the *Chicago Tribune* declared early on. Truman gleefully showed off a copy of this edition to reporters when later headlines told another tale. In America's most upset presidential-election victory, Harry Truman walked over Dewey, 303 electoral

A newly elected Harry Truman holds a copy of the Chicago Tribune, *which hastily declared Thomas E. Dewey the presidential winner in 1948. Election results were slow to come in on the night of November 2, 1948. With the printing deadline approaching, the remaining* Tribune *staff chose to go with the opinion of most media sources, which believed that Dewey would win. Thousands of copies of the paper were recalled the next morning, but this one found its way into Truman's hands in Saint Louis, Missouri.*

votes to 189, with 39 for Thurmond and none for Wallace. The sign in front of the *Washington Post* building summed it up. "Mr. President, we are ready to eat crow whenever you are ready to serve it."

During Truman's term, events in Korea and the Cold War threats of the Soviet Union pushed aside his programs of domestic reform. At home Truman's enemies ranted about Communist infiltration of the government, prompting Truman and Congress to establish the CIA (Central Intelligence Agency), an international spy agency.

When Communist North Korea invaded South Korea in June 1950, the president asked the United Nations (UN) for assistance. This organization of countries all around the world was created during Truman's first term to resolve global problems. Truman also sent U.S. ground troops to Asia during the Korean War (1950–1953). Americans blamed the president when the fighting stalemated, and Truman's popularity rating sank.

In March 1952, Truman announced he would not seek reelection. Ten months later, Citizen Truman left the White House for the final time. His spectacular whistle-stop tour shines in campaign history.

It was TV more than anything else that turned the tide.

—John F. Kennedy, commenting after the 1960 election

A cameraman films activities at the 1952 Republican National Convention.

STARRING ON THE SMALL SCREEN

PICTURE PERFECT

By 1952 television was becoming a fixture in most homes. In that year's election, for the first time ever during a convention, a national audience watched the candidates' addresses on TV. World War II hero general Dwight Eisenhower ran as the Republican nominee along with California senator Richard Nixon as the vice-presidential candidate. The Democrats nominated Illinois governor Adlai Stevenson.

During the contest, Eisenhower whistle-stopped by train—even traveled by plane—and stumped for votes. Of his electioneering experience, he wrote, "This campaign business is anything but easy. Life seems to be an unending round of engagements, conferences, discussions, arguments, and speeches. The most valuable thing the candidate possesses is his vocal cords. He can easily do without a brain—There are thousands ready to supply that commodity. But no one seems to have a ready cure for a sore throat."

To make sure Ike (Eisenhower's nickname) won, though, Republicans hired an advertising firm, the first time a national party ever did so. Ike's admen decided they would sell him to an audience already enthusiastically chanting, "I Like Ike."

Candidate Eisenhower popped up in television spot ads—political commercials—and addressed questions about war, taxes, and corruption. On TV Ike appeared to be an ordinary American, someone's grandfather.

Adlai Stevenson also posed for the cameras. In his nomination acceptance speech, he had said, "Let's talk sense to the American people." On TV he did just that. He was witty and intelligent. But his speeches droned on too long. To the public, Stevenson seemed

Adlai Stevenson (left) *speaks before a large crowd at the 1952 Democratic National Convention in Chicago, Illinois. The television cameras broadcast Stevenson's acceptance speech, which was considered smart and witty by some but too intellectual by others.*

like an "egghead," too brainy for everyday people. "You Never Had It So Good," his slogan, tried to convince the nation. But the voters weren't so sure about that. They linked him with another Democrat, the unpopular president, Harry Truman.

During his campaign, Ike attacked Truman's record. The president and his Democrats had brought "Korea, Corruption, and Communism," Eisenhower declared. In Asia, Communist North Korean forces continued to battle U.S.-backed South Korean troops with no sign of victory. In Washington some of the president's cronies had sold their influence and taken bribes. These included high-level officials in Truman's administration and personnel in the Internal Revenue Service. But even worse, Ike and the Republicans claimed, Communists overran the government and were out to destroy the nation.

With his war hero reputation and handful of issues, Eisenhower seemed unbeatable. Then came the rumors of illegal gifts of money accepted by his running mate, Richard Nixon.

On September 23, 1952, Nixon used television to defend himself before millions of viewers. The largest audience in TV history up

In 1952 Richard Nixon used the new medium of television to persuade millions of Americans that he was not, nor ever had been, involved in financial scandal.

until that time listened as the vice-presidential candidate explained that the money was legal. The only gift Nixon said he'd ever received was Checkers, a cocker spaniel, which he vowed to keep. Republican voters sympathized with him. They advised party leaders to keep him on the ticket, and Eisenhower agreed.

Toward the end of the campaign, Eisenhower spoke to his fellow citizens. "One tragedy challenges all men dedicated to the work of peace," he said. ". . . this tragedy . . . is: Korea. This is my pledge to the American people . . . I shall go to Korea." Americans realized Ike meant to resolve the deadlock and bring peace. The final tally on election eve registered a landslide win for the general, 442 electoral votes to Stevenson's 89.

In 1956 Republicans renominated Eisenhower, despite a recent heart attack and surgery. Again, he faced Adlai Stevenson.

The importance of primary elections had been diminishing for several years. The cost for holding such elections and the low voter turnout were partly responsible for this decline. Also, as the zest for reforming the United States had died down, voters didn't demand the same individual input. By 1956 primaries once again began to play a key role in presidential politics. Stevenson ran hard in the primaries to clinch his nomination.

As he began his race, he said, "The men who run the Eisenhower administration . . . believe that the minds of Americans can be manipulated by shows, slogans, and the arts of advertising. This idea that you can merchandise candidates for high office like breakfast cereal . . . is . . . the ultimate indignity to the democratic process." Then he asked voters to examine Ike's record.

As Ike had promised, he'd gone to Korea, and in 1953 the warring parties finally declared a truce. Even so, Americans still worried about the possibility of nuclear war with the Soviet Union.

At home the U.S. Supreme Court heard the arguments in a case called *Brown vs. the Board of Education of Topeka*. In its ruling, the Court decreed school segregation, the separation of black and white

Fulfilling a campaign pledge, president-elect Dwight Eisenhower (left) *visited U.S. troops in Korea in 1953.*

students, was illegal. This ruling overturned the *Plessy vs. Ferguson* (1896) decision that allowed "separate but equal" schools.

In 1955 Rosa Parks refused to give up her seat on a segregated bus in Montgomery, Alabama. Upon her arrest, the Reverend Martin Luther King Jr. led a boycott of the city's public transportation system. A year later, the Supreme Court also ordered an end to this type of segregation.

Just before the election, two world crises erupted. Egypt took control of the Suez Canal in Egypt, which linked the Mediterranean and Red Seas. According to an 1888 agreement, the waterway was to be open for trade to all nations. Britain, France, and Israel attacked Egypt. Before the crisis was resolved, the Soviet Union had threatened to become involved. In Europe, Hungarians revolted against the Soviet Union's rule. Both world situations posed a threat of war for the United States against the Soviet Union. Believing that Ike could keep the peace better than Stevenson could, the voters reelected him.

Eisenhower did not take a public stand on the segregation issue during his campaign for reelection, in 1957. But when the governor of Arkansas and the citizens of the state refused to desegregate Little Rock's Central High School, Ike sent in U.S. troops to enforce the law.

By 1960 Ike was nearing the end of his political career. However, television had just begun its hold on America.

DON'T TOUCH THAT DIAL

In 1960 the Democratic candidate, Massachusetts senator John F. Kennedy (JFK), was victorious in a series of primaries that clinched the Democratic nomination for him. He asked Lyndon B. Johnson (LBJ) of Texas to join him on the ticket.

During his acceptance speech, Kennedy talked about a New Frontier and the changes that awaited the country. "[W]e stand today on the edge of a New Frontier—the frontier of the 1960's—a frontier of unknown opportunities and perils—a frontier of unfilled hopes and threats," he said.

Senator Kennedy was energetic, wealthy, good looking, and a World War II hero. The voters, however, worried about his Catholic religion.

While Republican candidate Richard Nixon never attacked JFK's Catholicism, Americans again wondered whether a Roman Catholic would be loyal to the pope or the country, as they had when Al Smith ran for president. Meeting with a group of Protestant ministers in Houston, Texas, Kennedy assured them his allegiance lies with the United States. "I believe in an America where the separation of church and state is absolute," he said.

The public also fretted about Kennedy's age, forty-three, the youngest nominee ever. Nixon emphasized Kennedy's lack of experience and highlighted his own. He'd traveled overseas, met foreign dignitaries, and even visited with Soviet premier Nikita Khrushchev. He was a statesman who'd served as second in command for eight years.

To his critics, though, he was Tricky Dick, someone who couldn't be trusted. During his early campaigns, he had falsely accused his opponents of Communist leanings. He also still suffered from having to defend himself against charges of keeping a secret stash of campaign money during the 1952 vice-presidential race.

Nixon and Kennedy both stumped for votes. Traveling by plane, Nixon covered sixty-five thousand miles and kept his vow to visit each of the fifty states, including recently admitted Alaska and Hawaii. Kennedy trailed behind, touring forty-four states. Each candidate promised to make the United States a better country and to win the battle against Communism.

Like Eisenhower and Stevenson, the candidates sold themselves in television ads, in news specials, and on talk shows. But in this contest, for the first time ever, the two nominees appeared side by side as TV hosted the "Great Debates," four scheduled confrontations between the contenders. On September 26, 1960, a record 70 million viewers tuned in and watched John Kennedy versus Richard Nixon.

The two candidates discussed politics. But their stands on the issues didn't matter as much as the images that flickered across the screen. JFK was young, tanned, and confident. Richard Nixon thought he was a better debater than Kennedy, but Nixon was pale, thin, sweaty, with a hint of a beard, and he was suffering from a knee injury.

"Kennedy won!" his television fans insisted after the first debate. Radio listeners disagreed. They concentrated on words, not images, and most claimed Nixon the champ. The candidates faced off in three more debates not as widely watched as the first. Nixon began to give careful attention to his image.

The election that November was one of the closest in U.S. history. Sixty-four percent of the public voted. JFK won the popular vote, just barely (49.7 percent to 49.5 percent), but he edged Nixon electorally, 303 to 219. "It was TV more than anything else that turned the tide," Kennedy admitted.

Presidential candidates John F. Kennedy (left) and Richard M. Nixon (right) faced off during a series of televised debates in 1960. Nixon often looked stiff and frumpy compared to Kennedy during the debates.

John Kennedy took the oath of office on January 20, 1961. Soon after that, he learned that the Soviets had installed missiles in Cuba, an island in the Caribbean, just southeast of Florida. In October 1962, JFK quarantined Cuba by ordering a naval blockade of the island to prevent Communist enemies from shipping additional weapons there. Instead of starting nuclear war, Soviet leader Nikita Khrushchev ordered his ships to head for home.

During Kennedy's tenure, racial battles heated up too. In 1963 Sheriff "Bull" Connor of Birmingham, Alabama, turned fire hoses, cattle prods, and attack dogs on civil rights protesters. That same year, Martin Luther King Jr. headed a civil rights march on Washington, D.C., and delivered his "I have a dream" speech. JFK pushed for civil rights legislation.

Then, in Dallas on November 22, 1963, Lee Harvey Oswald shot and killed John F. Kennedy. As a stunned nation mourned his death, Vice President Lyndon Johnson took over.

Johnson worked hard to pass Kennedy's proposals, and in 1964 Democrats endorsed him as their presidential candidate. Of the upcoming race, Johnson would later say in his memoirs, "A political campaign is a blur, a whirlwind, an excitement—frustrating, exhilarating, and necessary."

Johnson had committed the United States to aiding South Vietnam in the Vietnam War (1957–1975) against Communist North Vietnam. In August 1964, Johnson reported that North Vietnam had attacked U.S. ships in the Gulf of Tonkin between Vietnam and China. He called for air strikes against the enemy and asked Congress to agree to a resolution allowing him to "take all necessary mea-

Following Kennedy's assassination, Lyndon Johnson (hand raised) *took the oath of office to become president of the United States in the cabin of Air Force One, the presidential plane, on November 22, 1963. On his left is Jacqueline Kennedy (JFK's widow) and on his right, his wife, Lady Bird.*

sures to repel any armed attack against the forces of the United States." Congress endorsed this Gulf of Tonkin Resolution. The United States was in a state of an undeclared war against North Vietnam. But Johnson insisted, "We are not going to send American boys away from home to do what Asian boys should be doing themselves."

Republicans nominated conservative Barry Goldwater, who believed in a smaller government that would not be involved in social issues. He also wanted to challenge the Soviet Union and its Communist allies. "I'd drop a low-yield atomic bomb on the Chinese supply lines in North Vietnam," he stated.

"In your heart, you know he's right," Goldwater's supporters insisted. "In your guts, you know he's nuts," Democrats retorted. Goldwater, they said, would push that button that would trigger war.

In an attempt to portray Goldwater as a warmonger, the Johnson campaign team aired a controversial television ad. In the forefront of the screen, a young girl peeled petals off a flower. In the background, as a voice counted backward from ten, a mushroom cloud appeared, the nuclear explosion that would destroy the world. "These are the stakes," Johnson then said. "We must either love each other or we must die."

Television advertising fueled a Johnson landslide. But just as television helped Johnson win, it also helped destroy his presidency. When Johnson sent U.S. ground troops to Vietnam, news anchors began to drone out counts of dead and wounded soldiers in the fighting. Images of war and of antiwar protesters chanting, "Hey! Hey, LBJ! How many kids did you kill today?" electrified the country. As Johnson tried to still the noise, the campaign of 1968 hovered in the distance.

Having lost a close one eight years ago, and having won a close one this year, I can say this— winning is a lot more fun.

—Richard Nixon, following his victory in 1968

A NEW WORLD AND THE OLD

DIRTY TRICKS

In 1968 Richard Nixon won the Republican nomination with Maryland governor Spiro Agnew as his running mate. In his acceptance speech, Nixon noted, "America is in trouble today, not because her people have failed but because her leaders have failed." He touched upon the war in Vietnam, the lawlessness that seemed to prevail in the United States, and racial violence. He concluded by offering his own leadership.

Lyndon Johnson had decided not to run again. As critics vehemently began to oppose his war policies, Johnson lost favor in the polls. He was also challenged in the primaries by Robert F. Kennedy, a New York senator and brother of John F. Kennedy, and Eugene McCarthy, a U.S. senator from Minnesota, both of whom called for peace in Vietnam.

At the Democratic convention, party leaders maneuvered to give Johnson's vice president, Hubert Humphrey, the nomination, although he'd entered no primaries. Robert Kennedy, his leading opponent, had been assassinated after the 1968 California primary. Humphrey, many believed, was tied to Johnson and would continue to support his war stand. Angry delegates fought over the Democratic platform, demanding an end to the bombing of North Vietnam and a withdrawal of the U.S. troops.

During the 1968 Democratic convention in Chicago, Humphrey spoke to the nation about Vietnam. "I pledge to you . . . that I will do everything within my power . . . to aid the negotiations and to bring a prompt end to this war!" he declared.

Still, chaos reigned on the streets of Chicago. Young antiwar demonstrators and agitators threw rocks and taunted cops. Americans watched on TV as the Chicago police, with their nightsticks, tear gas, and mace, charged at the protesters.

Antiwar protesters clashed with Chicago's police force on August 1, 1968, during the Democratic National Convention.

American Independent Party candidate George Wallace (right) mets with supporters in Texas during his campaign for president in 1968. His ideas appealed especially to white southerners who wished to preserve segregation.

During the campaign, Democrat Humphrey and Republican Nixon were joined by a third candidate, George Wallace. Wallace ran on the American Independent Party ticket and preached themes of law and order and segregation. The main issue of the campaign, however, was the Vietnam War. On the campaign trail, Humphrey dodged hecklers' insults. "Dump the Hump," they cried, sometimes not allowing him to finish speaking.

Richard Nixon didn't campaign nearly as much as his opponent. Instead, cameras filmed him at carefully screened and organized rallies and interviews, although hecklers bothered Nixon too. When Humphrey pressed Nixon to debate, he refused. Nixon hinted at a plan to end the war without offering specific suggestions, but the law-and-order themes he also stressed appealed to the Silent Majority of Americans. This Silent Majority, according to Nixon, referred to the Americans (the majority) who didn't riot, demonstrate, or attract attention with their opinions as the protesters (a minority of the population) did.

When Humphrey broke with Johnson's war strategy of bombing

North Vietnam and said he'd stop it, he moved up in the polls. On October 31, 1968, Lyndon Johnson himself stopped the bombing.

In a close race, Nixon was elected president. He received 43.4 percent of the popular vote to 42.7 percent for Humphrey with 13.5 percent going to Wallace. This translated to 301 electoral votes for Nixon to 191 for Humphrey and 46 for Wallace. "Having lost a close one eight years ago, and having won a close one this year, I can say this—winning is a lot more fun," he remarked. During Nixon's term, peace in Vietnam did not come. Still, at their 1972 convention, Republicans renominated him.

That year great changes occurred in the Democratic Party. Previously, convention delegates voted to choose one candidate from a group of several possible contenders. Sometimes it took several ballots to reach a decision, and party bosses or leaders frequently influenced the outcome. But in 1972, the number of states holding primaries increased, so the public had more voice in choosing among the candidates who had decided to run. In earlier races, most of the delegates to the convention had been selected by political chiefs. This time a large number were chosen in the primary races, and many were committed to a particular candidate.

Democrats had loosened their convention rules, and in 1972 women, minorities, and young people dominated the meeting. Before 1971 the legal voting age had been twenty-one. With the passage of the Twenty-Sixth Amendment to the Constitution in 1971, the age had been lowered to eighteen. These minority and younger voters favored George McGovern, who had won a string of primaries.

McGovern hoped to lure party leaders and everyday Americans when he addressed them at the convention. Few people heard him, however. Because of long internal party discussions, McGovern didn't speak until almost three in the morning.

Before McGovern began his campaign, he picked Thomas Eagleton as his running mate. McGovern didn't know Eagleton had been hospitalized for psychiatric problems that included emotional exhaustion and depression. He'd received electric shock treatments. When Eagleton's

George McGovern (left) *announces the withdrawal from the race of his first vice-presidential running mate, Thomas Eagleton* (right), *in July 1972. Eagleton was dropped from the Democratic Party ticket when his history of mental illness became public.*

past illness became public, McGovern said he was 1000 percent behind his choice. Then he dropped Eagleton from the ticket. Six potential candidates turned McGovern down before the seventh, Sargent Shriver, finally accepted the vice-presidential nomination.

On the stump, McGovern called for an end to the war and amnesty for draft dodgers. These young men had fled to Canada and other countries to escape being drafted or forced to serve in Vietnam in a war they felt was wrong.

Nixon, acting presidential, mostly stayed in the White House. His family and supporters stumped for him.

Behind the scenes, Richard Nixon behaved any way but presidential. He and his Committee to Reelect the President (CRP, jokingly known as CREEP) spread rumors and forged letters, spied against their opponents, and even directed the Internal Revenue Service (IRS) to audit tax returns of their opponents.

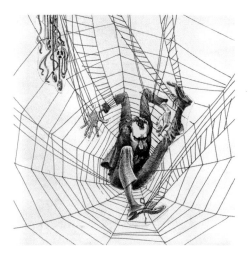

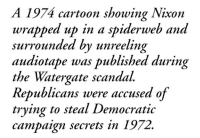

A 1974 cartoon showing Nixon wrapped up in a spiderweb and surrounded by unreeling audiotape was published during the Watergate scandal. Republicans were accused of trying to steal Democratic campaign secrets in 1972.

Then on June 17, 1972, police arrested five burglars caught breaking into Democratic national headquarters in the Watergate building complex in Washington, D.C. Several of them had close ties to CRP.

For the voting public, the Watergate break-in was an escapade, and it just didn't matter. When Nixon's foreign affairs adviser, Henry Kissinger, announced that peace in Vietnam was at hand, McGovern was seen as the candidate of antiwar agitators, young people, and minority rights groups. Nixon won in a landslide victory, 520 electoral votes to 17.

The United States pulled its troops out of Vientam in 1973. Nixon denied involvement in Watergate, but several of his aides were caught in lies and were headed to court. At the same time, Vice President Agnew was accused of accepting bribes and found guilty of tax evasion. He resigned from office in October 1973. The Twenty-Fifth Amendment (1967) to the Constitution called for the president to appoint a new vice president. U.S. representative Gerald Ford of Michigan took Agnew's place.

A Senate committee formed to investigate Nixon's part in the illegal Watergate activities. The committee learned that Nixon had installed a taping system inside his office, the Oval Office, to record his conversations. The committee called for the tapes. Nixon refused them over. In August 1974, the Supreme Court ordered the president to give up his tapes. Finally, Nixon obeyed. A stunned nation learned that its president had urged his staff to cover up and obstruct justice.

The House of Representatives Judiciary Committee approved three articles of impeachment against Nixon. If the House of Representatives voted its agreement with the committee, Nixon would be charged with obstructing justice and abusing his powers. Nixon faced almost certain removal from office. On August 8, 1974, Nixon resigned, the first president ever to do so. Gerald Ford became the first nonelected vice president to assume the presidency. On September 8, 1974, he pardoned Nixon for all crimes related to Watergate.

Even in the nineteenth century, parties needed money to pay for the costs of the races and to churn out literature extolling their candidates. Over the years, however, campaign spending mushroomed, and by the 1970s, it had spun out of control. Trying to curb the costs, new legislation passed in 1974 provided federal financing for presidential contests and set limits on the amount of money contributors could give to a candidate.

In 1976 Ford ran for the presidency against Democrat Jimmy Carter, a peanut farmer and one-term governor of Georgia. This race included a first-ever televised debate between the two vice-presidential candidates, Republican Robert Dole and Democrat Walter Mondale. And for the first time in sixteen years, the two presidential contenders also debated. Jimmy Carter eked out the win.

NOW WHAT?

By 1980 a company of advisers, consultants, fund-raisers, and specialists surrounded the nominees. As the contenders pursued victory, they participated in primary contests, advertising, national debates, and old-fashioned stumping. All had become standard fare in presidential politicking. TV wove these separate elements together and brought the candidates directly to the voters.

"WHO'S IN CHARGE HERE?"

In a political cartoon from 1979, President Carter stands in front of the desk in the Oval Office holding a Visitor's Guide to Washington *and demanding to know, "Who's in charge here?"*

A 1979 Herblock Cartoon, copyright by The Herb Block Foundation

The election that year featured President Jimmy Carter against Republican Ronald Reagan, a one-time actor, former California governor, and at sixty-nine, the oldest presidential candidate ever. Reagan often butchered the facts, once saying trees caused more pollution than cars. In his convention acceptance speech, however, Reagan emphasized Carter's missteps as president. "I will not stand by and watch this great country destroy itself under mediocre leadership that drifts from one crisis to the next. Can anyone look at the record of this administration and say, 'Well done'?" he asked.

After four Carter years, the nation was in an economic slump that included high inflation and high unemployment. The Organization of Petroleum Exporting Countries (OPEC), retaliating for U.S. support of Israel in its 1973 war against Arab nations, cut their shipments of oil to the United States. Americans waited in long lines to purchase what gas they could. In Tehran, Iran, students held fifty-two U.S. citizens hostage. The students demanded the return of the shah, their former leader, to face justice for his misdeeds as ruler. The U.S.-supported shah was in the United States for medical treatment, and Carter had led a failed attempt to rescue the hostages.

Jimmy Carter tried to convince voters to reelect him. At the Democratic convention, he reminded his audience, "This election is a stark choice between two men . . . two sharply different pictures of what America is . . . it's a choice between two futures."

However, in their nationally televised debate, Reagan, often called the Great Communicator, faced the camera and asked his viewers, "Are you better off than you were four years ago?" No, they concluded and handed Reagan a win. John Anderson of the National Unity Party took 6.6 percent of the popular vote.

In 1984 Republicans renominated Reagan. He ran against Carter's vice president, Walter Mondale. During the campaign, Reagan's "Morning in America" TV ads stressed old-fashioned values and patriotism. The country basked in Reagan's vision of a peaceful and prosperous country. The president won a stunning victory—forty-nine of fifty states, with 525 electoral votes to 13 electoral votes for Mondale.

Still, during his term, Reagan became mired in controversy. A secret deal approved the selling of armaments to Iran, an enemy of the United States, as a bribe to free Americans held hostage in Lebanon by Iranian supporters. Selling of arms to terrorist nations was against U.S. policy. The money gained from the sale was passed on to the Contras, a group in Nicaragua who were fighting their Communist-leaning government, even though Congress had previously refused to send such aid to the Contras. Congressional hearings into the Iran-Contra scandal later determined that Reagan had not personally been involved.

In 1988, with Reagan ineligible to run again, Republicans nominated Vice President George H. W. Bush. He ran against Massachusetts governor Michael Dukakis.

The Bush race featured negative campaigning to demean or smear its opponent. As governor, Dukakis had authorized a state prison furlough plan. Under the plan, a prisoner named Willie Horton had been

Gov 'gave pardons to 21 drug dealers'

Will Dukakis Turn Gun Owners Into Criminals... While Murderers Go Free?

The Most Soft-on-Crime Governor in Massachusetts History
Is a Leading Advocate of Gun Control

Gun Owner Magazine quotes Dukakis as saying in 1986, **"I don't believe in people owning guns, only the police and military. And I'm going to do everything I can to disarm this state."** In 1976 Dukakis supported a (losing) statewide referendum which would have done just that. Dukakis has called for **federal registration** of all concealable handguns and has written, "... the solution to the problem of gun-inflicted violence must come at the national level."

Michael Dukakis talks about fighting crime, but there is a big gap between the *rhetoric* and the *record*. Maybe that's why the **Boston Police Patrolman's Association** unanimously endorsed George Bush for President.

While trying to deny the citizens of Massachusetts the right to defend themselves, Dukakis has put more convicted criminals on the streets than any governor in his state's history.

• He has used his gubernatorial pardoning power to commute the sentences of 44 *convicted murderers*—a record for the state of Massachusetts.

• He has vetoed and continues to oppose the death penalty *under any circumstances*, even for cop-killers, drug kingpins and traitors.

• He *opposes* mandatory sentences for hard-core criminals but *supports* mandatory sentences for anyone caught with an unregistered gun of *any kind*.

Dukakis has also presided over and actively endorsed the *most liberal prisoner furlough program in America*, the **only one in the nation** releasing prisoners sentenced to life without parole.

• On average, in the state of Massachusetts, one convicted first degree murderer was released *every day* over the last seven years.

• Since the beginning of Dukakis's second term as Governor, 1,905 furloughs have been granted to first degree murderers and at least 4,459 furloughs to second degree murderers. He has given 2,565 furloughs to drug offenders.

• In 1986 alone, Dukakis gave 1,229 furloughs to sex crime offenders, including 220 to persons charged with *six or more* sex offenses.

• Today **85 violent felons from Massachusetts are on the loose** in America—set free on furloughs, they never bothered to come back.

Meet Willie Horton.

Willie Horton was convicted in 1975 and sentenced to life in prison without parole for stabbing a 17-year-old to death during a robbery. In 1986, on his tenth release under the Dukakis-supported furlough program, he escaped to Maryland where he stabbed and beat a man and then repeatedly raped his fiancee.

Horton was captured, but Maryland Judge Vincent Femia refused to send him back to Massachusetts saying, "I am not prepared to take the chance that Mr. Horton might be furloughed or otherwise released ...

I would strongly urge the people of Massachusetts not to wait up for Mr. Horton ... not to bother to put out a light for him because he won't be coming home." Judge Femia recommended that Horton, "should never draw a breath of free air again ... and should die in prison." Michael Dukakis refused to even meet with the parents of the couple Horton attacked, saying, "I don't see any particular value in meeting with people ... I'm satisfied ... we have the kind of furlough policy we should have."

As part of the negative 1988 campaign against Massachusets governor Michael Dukakis, Republicans ran newspaper ads featuring convicted murderer Willie Horton. He had been released through Dukakis's prison furlough (temporary leave-of-absence) plan and committed more crimes.

released. While free, he sexually assaulted a woman and stabbed her male companion. Bush supporters splashed Horton's mug shot over the TV screens and blamed Dukakis for Horton's crimes. They insisted Dukakis was soft on crime. Dukakis did not rebut the charges and, instead, seemed on the defensive. Such mean-spirited advertising fueled Bush's win, and he became the first sitting vice president to be elected to the White House since Martin Van Buren in 1836.

During Bush's term, the Soviet Union had dissolved, ending the Cold War. In the Middle East, Iraq invaded Kuwait, claiming unresolved disagreements between the two nations. Other world powers, with an eye on Mideast oil reserves, worried about a possible expanded war. Bush organized and led a coalition of nations in a war against Iraq, which included both bombing and ground troops. Iraq was forced to withdraw from Kuwait, and the coalition declared victory.

In 1992 George H. W. Bush ran for reelection against Democratic governor Bill Clinton of Arkansas. Clinton, on the other hand, spoke to the middle classes about issues that appealed to them, especially a sagging economy.

On the stump, Clinton and vice-presidential candidate Al Gore boarded a specially designed bus and toured small towns. By 1992 coverage on cable television, talk shows, and call-in programs offered the United States a less formal picture of all the candidates. Clinton, an expert and enthusiastic campaigner, took to the TV and radio circuit. On one late-night TV show, he donned dark glasses and played the saxophone. Hoping to appeal to younger generations, he appeared on MTV, a music video television network.

In a series of three-way, televised debates in 1992, presidential candidates (**from left to right**) *Republican George H. W. Bush, independent H. Ross Perot, and Democrat Bill Clinton compared their political views on the issues.*

Again, television aired the debates. These 1992 sessions introduced a third candidate, independent H. Ross Perot. Perot was a popular choice early on. For voters tired of the major party candidates, Perot presented a different choice. He also talked about a major issue—reducing the national debt. In July 1992, however, he dropped out of the race. It might have been because the media was examining his life closely. Or perhaps it was because Clinton's ratings had jumped, and he became a more competitive opponent. Perot reentered the race in October. With his name on fifty ballots, he joined the two major party candidates on national TV.

Some voters disliked Clinton. They called him Slick Willie. He was smooth talking, seemed manipulative, and was plagued by sex scandals. But many voters were desperate for a change. On election day, they gave Clinton the win, 370 electoral votes and 43 percent of the popular vote to 168 electoral votes and 37 percent of the popular vote for Bush. Perot's third party scored well with 19 percent of the popular vote but received no electoral votes.

By the end of Clinton's first term, the U.S. economy was booming. In 1996 Clinton ran against Republican Robert Dole of Kansas. Dole's age and what some called Clinton's shady character were issues that caused some concern. Each side avoided negative advertising. Clinton ran as a centrist and appealed to the middle class. In November he was again elected president. He became the first Democrat since Franklin Roosevelt to be reelected.

Clinton's second term was marred by scandal. For the first time since 1868, the House of Representatives voted to impeach a president. They charged Clinton with obstruction of justice and perjury in connection with his sexual relationship with a White House intern. Following a Senate trial, Clinton was acquitted on both charges.

Television was now in the foreground of presidential campaigning. But technology was developing rapidly, bringing new changes to daily life and on the campaign trail as well. What would the future bring for those courageous enough to run for office?

I loved campaigning. I did seven, eight events a day. I never left until I had shaken every hand.

—John Kerry, on Campaign 2004

Democratic candidate John Kerry (left) talks with comedian Billy Crystal during a campaign fund-raiser in 2004.

THE NEW CENTURY

DEADLOCK

In 2000 Vice President Al Gore and Texas governor George W. Bush, son of former president George H. W. Bush, vied for the presidency. Each had amassed enough primary delegates committed to voting for them to be officially nominated at the summer conventions.

In his nomination acceptance speech, Gore established that he was not merely President Clinton's shadow. "We're entering a new time," he said. "We're electing a new president. And I stand here tonight as my own man." George W. Bush also addressed several key themes: "We will confront the hard issues, threats to our national security, threats to our health and retirement security, before the challenges . . . become crises for our children."

Both candidates plunged into the race. Neither one a reluctant candidate, Gore and Bush sponsored positive and negative television ads, stumped the nation, talked to citizens, and faced each other in three debates.

All along, pollsters had predicted the race would be close. On election eve, it came down to Florida's electoral votes. Each candidate needed Florida's votes to win. When newscasters declared a Bush victory in Florida—Bush's brother Jeb was Florida's governor—Gore contacted George Bush to concede. In politics it is a tradition that the one who loses a race calls the victor to admit defeat. But Florida's final vote had been so close that Florida law demanded an automatic recount. The state's election code calls for a recount in cases where a candidate loses by one-half of 1 percent or less. So Gore called Bush

Republican George W. Bush (left) *and Democrat Al Gore* (right) *shared their views with the nation in the second televised presidential debate at Wake Forest University in North Carolina in October 2000.*

again to tell him that the circumstances had changed.

"Let me make sure that I understand you. You're calling back to retract that concession?" Bush asked.

"You don't have to be snippy about it," Gore answered.

With a recount accomplished, Gore trailed by only 327 votes. However, on election day, his advisers had heard complaints about Florida voting. The "butterfly ballot" had confused many voters. This two-page document with punch holes down the center listed ten presidential candidates. Many voters said it was difficult to read. In Palm Beach County, with heavy support for Gore, they worried that they'd voted for the wrong man. African Americans reported that they'd been turned away from the polls. Gore and his attorneys asked for a recount by hand in several disputed counties.

The boards in Volusia, Broward, Miami-Dade, and Palm Beach counties reviewed Gore's request. Broward and Miami-Dade refused to recount the votes. Volusia agreed to a recount and completed its

A political cartoon from the 2000 presidential election highlights the confusion stirred up in attempting to recount ballots in Florida.

task. Palm Beach also decided to recount. Florida law requires certification of election results within seven days of an election. Florida's Republican secretary of state refused to extend that deadline.

Al Gore worried that a recount would not be completed by the deadline, so his attorneys headed to court. The Florida Supreme Court finally ruled that the recounts could continue and set as the new certification date November 26, 5:00 P.M.

A second controversy also brewed in Florida. Without a legal postmark, a marking that indicates the date and time a letter is received by the postal service, overseas votes (a large number from military personnel) were invalid. But Bush's team believed that all military votes should be counted whether they were legally marked or not. The Democrats finally agreed. With strong military support for Bush, the overseas votes jumped Bush's lead by several hundred.

The county boards continued to count. On November 22, however, Miami-Dade stopped in midtask. Republican protesters had been demonstrating noisily outside while the vote counters worked inside. The Miami-Dade board said it would not be able to meet the deadline.

On November 26, the Florida secretary of state certified George W. Bush the winner of Florida's presidential race by 537 votes. The final Florida count was 2,912,790 for Bush to 2,912,253 for Gore. Broward County had submitted its results. Palm Beach missed the deadline by two hours.

In court again, Gore's team wanted the under votes, those ballots with no clear choice marked, double-checked. On December 4, the court ruled against Gore's request. On that same day, the U.S. Supreme Court sent Bush's appeal to stop the recounts back to Florida's Supreme Court.

Besides clarifying their decision, Florida's justices listened to another appeal from Gore's lawyers. Then they ruled to allow a manual recount of all the state's under votes, but they didn't explain how to judge what was an acceptable under vote.

On December 10, 1999, the U.S. Supreme Court ordered all

recounting stopped. On December 12, the Court announced that the problem was equal protection. Without a standard for judging votes, they meant something different in each county. They were not equal. There were to be no additional recounts, the Court concluded. With that, George W. Bush took Florida's electoral votes and the presidency, even though Gore had won the national popular vote. In order to avoid a repeat of the 2000 election mess, Congress passed the Help America Vote Act in 2002. This bill required local governments to use voting machines that met certain set standards. According to some experts, however, the new electronic machines cause their own problems. Many do not leave a paper audit trail, a written accounting. This would create new difficulties should a recount be necessary.

On December 13, Al Gore called president-elect George W. Bush to concede, and Gore, this time, did not retract his words. Then he spoke to the nation. "Let there be no doubt," Gore emphasized, "while I strongly disagree with the Court's decision, I accept it. And tonight, for the sake of our unity . . . and the strength of our democracy, I offer my concession." These words marked the final page in the story of Election 2000.

MONEY TALKS

On September 11, 2001, nineteen Islamic extremists highjacked four U.S. commercial airplanes. They flew two of them into the twin towers of New York's World Trade Center and one into the Pentagon, the armed services office building near Washington, D.C. Passengers on the fourth jet attempted to overpower the terrorists, and it crashed into a Pennsylvania field. Almost three thousand people died in the aftermath of these attacks.

President Bush denounced al-Qaeda, the Islamic network that had organized this violence. He sent U.S. forces to Afghanistan, which had offered al-Qaeda a haven. They quickly overthrew the Islamic Taliban government there that had harbored al-Qaeda.

In March 2003, Bush began a war on Iraq. He claimed that its leader, Saddam Hussein, had amassed weapons of mass destruction that could be used against the United States. Repeatedly explaining his actions, Bush insisted that the United States must strike at terrorists around the world rather than confront them on its own soil.

Although no weapons of mass destruction were ever found, Saddam's regime was toppled. In the aftermath, insurgents continued to target Iraqi citizens and U.S. troops still in the country.

In 2004 George W. Bush ran for reelection as a wartime president. To oppose him, Democrats nominated Massachusetts senator John Kerry. Unlike the president, who had served in the National Guard and seen no combat, Kerry was a decorated Vietnam War veteran.

Iraq and the threat of terror were major issues in the contest. John Kerry, like many others in Congress, had originally supported Bush's call for military action. During the campaign, though, he began to criticize the president's handling of the crisis stating, "It is the wrong war at the wrong place in the wrong time."

Bush and his supporters lashed out at his opponent. They quoted Kerry's own words: "I actually did vote for the $87 billion [to finance the war] before I voted against it," and they called him a flip-flopper. "Senator Kerry's been in Washington long enough to take both sides on just about every issue," Bush said.

The most effective way for campaigns to spread their messages to the most people is through television ads. Both parties used huge chunks of their budgets to fund such advertising.

The Bipartisan Campaign Reform Act of 2002, also known as the McCain-Feingold Bill, put new controls on moneys donated during a campaign. Part of the legislation limited what cash the political parties could accept. Still, in 2004 raising money was a top priority during both the primary and general election seasons. Campaign teams solicited money for their candidates from large donors and from political action committees, PACs. Business corporations and labor organizations are not permitted by law to give money to a campaign.

To circumvent the law, these groups can form PACs, which contribute the money instead. Direct mailing, an effective tool since the 1960s, drew money from small donors.

In this contest, modern technology also brought new ways of taking in cash. Howard Dean, a Democratic primary candidate and former Vermont governor, started a trend by using the Internet to ask for contributions. Visitors to Dean's website were invited to donate to his campaign. He received most of his moneys through small donations (many under eighty dollars). Deaniacs, as his supporters were called, also used Internet blogs—online journals—to share information and ideas, a technique the Bush team later adopted.

As a result of the Bipartisan Campaign Reform Act, special interest groups played a major role in the 2004 race. These groups, called 527s (referring to a tax form), could not directly support a candidate, but they could raise money to sponsor advertising about issues. While their ads sometimes supported issues of a preferred candidate, more

Howard Dean revolutionized the way campaign financing was done by soliciting contributions through his Internet website during his bid for the 2004 Democratic nomination for president.

often they viciously attacked his opponent. The 527s for Bush, especially the Swift Boat Veterans for Truth, ran negative ads throwing doubt on how Kerry had earned his navy medals and implying that he was no hero.

John Kerry tried to mold his own image. In his nomination acceptance speech, he had said, "I defended this country as a young man and I will defend it as a president." As to the threat of terror, he added, "Let there be no mistake. I will never hesitate to use force when it is required. Any attack will be met with a swift and certain response."

On the stump, especially toward the end of his race and in the three debates against Bush, Kerry became more emphatic about his message. Still, the Swift Boat ads weakened Kerry's assertions that he would be tough on terrorism. Many voters were convinced that Bush would be stronger against terror. They also believed Bush deserved support because it might be dangerous to change leaders during wartime. Others felt that Bush represented them on issues of moral and family values. As a result, the president won the election, 286 electoral votes to 251. (In the formal voting of the Electoral College, one Democratic elector cast presidential and vice-presidential ballots for the same man, John Edwards, John Kerry's running mate.)

Even as Bush took the oath of office, a band of presidential hopefuls was hatching future plans. Americans watched George W. Bush's inaugural and waited for Campaign 2008 to begin.

WHO WILL RUN?

Since the earliest races, white men have dominated presidential politics and have excluded women and minorities. Still, a daring few ignored those taboos. In 1872 Victoria Woodhull became the first woman ever to enter a race for the highest office as candidate of the Equal Rights Party. Woodhull, outspoken and given to radical views, alienated many, including other women pressing for universal suffrage. Her run came to a quick end because of personal and legal

Victoria Woodhull (left) *and Belva Lockwood* (right) *broke the gender barrier in politics by running for the nation's top office in the 1800s.*

problems. In the weekly paper she had established, Woodhull exposed the Reverend Henry Ward Beecher for an illicit affair he was rumored to be having. Woodhull was charged with sending obscene material through the mail and was arrested.

Belva Lockwood was a women's suffrage leader who pressed to have legislation enacted that would allow women to practice law before the Supreme Court. At that time, women were not permitted to do so. Not only did she then become the first woman to go before the Court, she also ran for president on the National Equal Rights Party ticket in 1884. "Why not nominate women for important places?" she once wrote. "Is not [the queen of England] Empress of India? Have we not among our own country women persons of as much talent and ability? Is not history full of precedents of women rulers? . . . It is time we had our own party, our own platform, and our own nominees." Although Lockwood spoke on her own behalf and drew some support, many laughed at her candidacy. She didn't win, but she did receive over four thousand votes. In 1888 Lockwood made a second run for the White House, but did not do as well as she had earlier.

In the changing cultural climate of the mid-twentieth century, women and minorities came to play a larger role in national politics. Republican Margaret Chase Smith of Maine, who had served in both the House and the Senate, campaigned for president in two state primaries in 1964. She lost both. The majority of voters did not take her run seriously. She was nominated at the Republican convention that year and received twenty-seven delegate votes.

In 1972 Shirley Chisholm, the first African American woman elected to Congress, announced her bid for the presidency. "I stand before you today as a candidate for the Democratic nomination for the Presidency of the United States. I am not the candidate of black America, although I am black and proud. I am not the candidate of the women's movement of this country, although I am a woman, and I am equally proud of that. I am not the candidate of any political bosses or special interests. I am the candidate of the people." Chisholm, the first black woman to run on a major party, failed to

Shirley Chisholm was a New York congresswoman before being elected to the U.S. House of Representatives in 1968. In 1972 she became the first African American candidate for president. She didn't win the Democratic Party's nomination, but she helped pave the way for future women and minorities to run for president.

In July 1984, Democrat Walter Mondale introduced Geraldine Ferraro as his running mate.

receive the nomination but won 151 votes at the convention.

In 1984 Democratic nominee Walter Mondale chose New York congresswoman Geraldine Ferraro for his running mate. She was the first woman featured on a major party ticket. The Mondale-Ferraro ticket lost, however, as incumbent Ronald Reagan won a landslide victory.

That same year, minority voices grew louder. Jesse Jackson Sr., an African American civil rights activist from Illinois, ran for the Democratic presidential nomination. Jackson won a handful of primaries and received 3.5 million votes in these contests. During the primary season, he came in third in the voting, behind Mondale and Senator Gary Hart of Colorado. In 1988 Jackson ran again in the primaries, doing even better. He took a string of primaries, including Michigan and the southern states of Louisiana and Alabama. Jackson received close to 7 million votes and claimed over 1,200 delegates. Still, he lost the nomination to Michael Dukakis.

Just as gender and racial barriers had begun to break down, so too did religious ones. John Kennedy had been the first Roman Catholic to reach the presidency in 1960. In 2000 Democratic candidate Al Gore tapped Joe Lieberman, a U.S. senator from Connecticut and the first Jew nominated as a running mate. Although the Democratic team lost to George W. Bush, Lieberman ran for his party's presidential nomination in the 2004 primaries. Failing to come up with a win, he dropped out of the race. In that same year, two African Americans, a man and a woman, also threw their hats into the ring, the Reverend Al Sharpton of New York and former U.S. senator Carol Moseley Braun of Illinois. Neither candidate was a front-runner in the race.

As the next election looms, Americans may wonder: Will the parties follow tradition and nominate a man? Or will they travel a different road? Who will run? A woman? An African American? A Jew or a Hispanic? In the twenty-first century in presidential politics, the doors are open.

Senators Hillary Rodham Clinton of New York (left), *wife of former president Bill Clinton, and Barack Obama of Illinois* (right) *campaigned hard in 2007 for a chance to be chosen as the Democratic Party's candidate for U.S. president in 2008.*

ELECTION RESULTS

This chart shows the percentage of popular votes for each of the major candidates in U.S. presidential elections from early nationhood until the presidential election in 2004.

Year Candidates	Electoral Vote	% of Popular Vote	Year Candidates	Electoral Vote	% of Popular Vote
1789			**1840**		
George Washington	69		William H. Harrison	234	53%
John Adams	34		Martin Van Buren	60	47%
1792			**1844**		
George Washington	132		James K. Polk	170	50%
John Adams	77		Henry Clay	105	48%
1796			**1848**		
John Adams	71		Zachary Taylor	163	47%
Thomas Jefferson	68		Lewis Cass	127	43%
1800			Martin Van Buren	0	10%
Thomas Jefferson	73		**1852**		
John Adams	65		Franklin Pierce	254	51%
1804			Winfield Scott	42	44%
Thomas Jefferson	162		**1856**		
Charles C. Pinckney	14		James Buchanan	174	45%
1808			John C. Frémont	114	33%
James Madison	122		Millard Fillmore	8	22%
Charles C. Pinckney	47		**1860**		
1812			Abraham Lincoln	180	40%
James Madison	128		Stephen A. Douglas	12	29%
DeWitt Clinton	89		John C. Breckinridge	72	18%
1816			John Bell	39	13%
James Monroe	183		**1864**		
Rufus King	34		Abraham Lincoln	212	55%
1820			George B. McClellan	21	45%
James Monroe	231		**1868**		
1824			Ulysses S. Grant	214	53%
John Quincy Adams	84	31%	Horatio Seymour	80	47%
Andrew Jackson	99	43%	**1872**		
William Crawford	41	13%	Ulysses S. Grant	286	56%
Henry Clay	37	13%	Horace Greeley	66	44%
1828			**1876**		
Andrew Jackson	178	56%	Rutherford B. Hayes	185	48%
John Quincy Adams	83	44%	Samuel J. Tilden	184	51%
1832			**1880**		
Andrew Jackson	219	55%	James Garfield	214	48.5%
Henry Clay	49	42%	Winfield S. Hancock	155	48.1%
1836			**1884**		
Martin Van Buren	170	51%	Grover Cleveland	219	49%
William H. Harrison	73	36%	James G. Blaine	182	48%
Hugh L. White	26	10%	**1888**		
Daniel Webster	14	3%	Benjamin Harrison	233	48%
			Grover Cleveland	168	49%
			1892		
			Grover Cleveland	277	46%
			Benjamin Harrison	145	43%
			James B. Weaver	22	9%

1896		
William McKinley	271	51%
William J. Bryan	176	47%

1900		
William McKinley	292	52%
William J. Bryan	155	46%

1904		
Theodore Roosevelt	336	56%
Alton B. Parker	140	38%

1908		
William H. Taft	321	52%
William J. Bryan	162	43%

1912		
Woodrow Wilson	435	42%
Theodore Roosevelt	88	27%
William H. Taft	8	23%

1916		
Woodrow Wilson	277	49%
Charles E. Hughes	254	46%

1920		
Warren G. Harding	404	61%
James M. Cox	127	35%

1924		
Calvin Coolidge	382	54%
John W. Davis	136	29%
Robert M. LaFollette	13	17%

1928		
Herbert C. Hoover	444	58%
Alfred E. Smith	87	41%

1932		
Franklin D. Roosevelt	472	57%
Herbert C. Hoover	59	40%

1936		
Franklin D. Roosevelt	523	61%
Alfred M. Landon	8	37%

1940		
Franklin D. Roosevelt	449	55%
Wendell L. Willkie	82	45%

1944		
Franklin D. Roosevelt	432	53%
Thomas E. Dewey	99	46%

1948		
Harry S. Truman	303	49%
Thomas E. Dewey	189	45%
Strom Thurmond	39	2%
Henry A. Wallace	0	2%

1952		
Dwight Eisenhower	442	55%
Adlai E. Stevenson	89	44%

1956		
Dwight Eisenhower	457	57%
Adlai E. Stevenson	73	42%

1960		
John F. Kennedy	303	49.7%
Richard M. Nixon	219	49.5%

1964		
Lyndon B. Johnson	486	61%
Barry Goldwater	52	39%

1968		
Richard M. Nixon	301	43.4%
Hubert H. Humphrey	191	42.7%
George C. Wallace	46	13.5%

1972		
Richard M. Nixon	520	61%
George McGovern	17	8%

1976		
Jimmy Carter	297	50%
Gerald Ford	240	48%

1980		
Ronald Reagan	489	51%
Jimmy Carter	49	41%
John B. Anderson	0	7%

1984		
Ronald Reagan	525	41%
Walter F. Mondale	13	59%

1988		
George H. W. Bush	426	54%
Michael S. Dukakis	111	46%

1992		
Bill Clinton	370	43%
George H. W. Bush	168	37%
Ross Perot	0	19%

1996		
Bill Clinton	379	49%
Robert Dole	159	41%
Ross Perot	0	8%

2000		
George W. Bush	271	48%
Al Gore	266	48%

2004		
George W. Bush	286	51%
John Kerry	251	48%

SOURCE NOTES

5 Paul Leicester Ford, ed., *The Works of Thomas Jefferson*, vol. 9 (New York: G. P. Putnam's Sons, 1905), 155.

7 H. A. Washington, ed., *The Writings of Thomas Jefferson: Being His Autobiography, Correspondence, Reports, Messages, Addresses, and Other Writings, Official and Private, vol. 4* (Washington, DC: Taylor & Maury, 1854), 151.

8 Ibid., 153.

9 Ford, *The Works of Thomas Jefferson*, 155.

11 Harold D. Moser, David R. Hoth, and George H. Hoemann, eds., *The Papers of Andrew Jackson: 1821–1828*, vol. 5 (Knoxville: University of Tennessee Press, 1996), 383.

11 Ibid., 382.

13 Paul F. Boller Jr., *Presidential Campaigns* (New York: Oxford University Press, 1984), 36.

13 Charles Francis Adams, ed., *Memoirs of John Quincy Adams: Comprising Portions of His Diary From 1795–1848*, vol. 6 (New York: AMS Press, 1970), 502.

15 Adams, *Memoirs of John Quincy Adams, 7:76.*

15 Ibid.

17 Ibid., 78.

20 John C. Fitzpatrick, ed., *The Autobiography of Martin Van Buren* (New York: Augustus M. Kelley, 1969), 769.

21 Kirk H. Porter and Donald Bruce Johnson, eds., *National Party Platforms 1840–1964* (Urbana: University of Illinois Press, 1966), 2.

21 A. B. Norton, *Reminiscences of the Log Cabin and Hard Cider Campaign* (Mount Vernon, OH: A. B. Norton & Co., 1888), 289–290.

22 Boller, *Presidential Campaigns*, 67.

23 Evan Cornog and Richard Whelan, *Hats in the Ring: An Illustrated History of American Presidential Campaigns* (New York: Random House, 2000), 104.

23 Wayne Cutler, ed., *Correspondence of James K. Polk, Jan.–Aug. 1844,* vol. 7 (Nashville: Vanderbilt University Press, 1989), 221.

24 Melba Porter Hay, ed., *The Papers of Henry Clay: Candidate, Compromiser, Elder Statesman, January 1, 1844–June 29, 1852,* vol. 10 (Lexington: University Press of Kentucky, 1991), 149.

28 Carl Sandburg, *Abraham Lincoln: The Prairie Years and the War Years* (New York: Harcourt, Brace & World, 1954), 181.

29 Marvin R. Weisbord, *Campaigning for President: A Look at the Road to the White House* (New York: Washington Square Press, 1966), 267.

30 Eileen Shields-West, *The World Almanac of Presidential Campaigns* (New York: World Almanac, 1992), 85.

30 Cornog and Whelan, *Hats in the Ring*, 112.

31 *New York Times*, June 10, 1864, 1.

32 Gil Troy, *See How They Ran: The Changing Role of the Presidential Candidate* (New York: Free Press, 1991), 73.

32 Cornog and Whelan, *Hats in the Ring*, 116.

32 Porter and Johnson, *National Party Platforms 1840–1964*, 38.

33 *The World Book Encyclopedia*, "Constitution of the United States." ed., s.v.

33 Troy, *See How They Ran*, 73.

34 Arthur M. Schlesinger Jr., ed., *Running for President: The Candidates and Their Images 1789–1896*, vol. 1 (New York: Simon & Schuster, 1994), 328.

35 Troy, *See How They Ran*, 78.

35 Historian's Office, National Portrait Gallery, *"If Elected . . . ": Unsuccessful Candidates for the Presidency 1796–1968* (Washington, DC: Smithsonian Institution Press, 1972), 229.

37 Ibid., 237.

38 Troy, *See How They Ran*, 95.

40 Historian's Office, *If Elected*, 271.

41 Schlesinger, *Running for President,* 2:49.

41 Weisbord, *Campaigning for President*, 286.

42 Cornog and Whelan, *Hats in the Ring*, 158.

42 Shields-West, *The World Almanac of Presidential Campaigns*, 129.

44 Schlesinger, *Running for President*, 2:49.

45 Cornog and Whelan, *Hats in the Ring*, 179.

45 *New York Times*, June 23, 1912, A1.

45 Boller, *Presidential Campaigns*, 193.

46 *New York Times*, August 8, 1912, A6.

46 Boller, *Presidential Campaigns*, 194.

47 James M. McPherson, ed., *To the Best of My Ability: The American Presidents* (New York: Dorling Kindersley, 2000), 203.

49 Alfred E. Smith, *Up to Now: An Autobiography* (New York: Viking Press, 1929), 391.

49 Aaron Singer, *Campaign Speeches of American Presidential Candidates 1928–1972* (New York: Frederick Ungar Publishing Company, 1976), 7.

50 Ibid., 62.

50 Herbert Hoover, *The Memoirs of Herbert Hoover: The Cabinet and the Presidency 1920–1933* (New York: MacMillan Company, 1951), 199.

50 Smith, *Up to Now*, 391.

50 McPherson, *To the Best of My Ability*, 415.

51 Singer, *Campaign Speeches of American Presidential Candidates 1928–1972*, 68.

54 Boller, *Presidential Campaigns*, 271.

54 Porter and Johnson, *National Party Platforms 1840–1964*, 435.

55 Weisbord, *Campaigning for President*, 361, 365.

56 McPherson, *To the Best of My Ability*, 423.

58 Troy, *See How They Ran*, 214.

58 Louis Galambos, ed., *The Papers of Dwight David Eisenhower: Nato and the Campaign of 1952,* vol. 13 (Baltimore: Johns Hopkins University, 1989), 1,356.

59 Singer, *Campaign Speeches of American Presidential Candidates 1928–1972*, 253.

60 Ibid., 245.

60 Ibid., 284.

62 Ibid., 302.

62 Shields-West, *The World Almanac of Presidential Campaigns*, 206.

63 Troy, *See How They Ran*, 214.

64 Lyndon Baines Johnson, *The Vantage Point: Perspectives of the Presidency 1963–1969* (New York: Holt, Rinehart and Winston, 1971), 105.

64 Cornog and Whelan, *Hats in the Ring*, 259.

64 Ibid., 262.

65 *The World Book Encyclopedia,* ed., s.v. "Vietnam War."

65 Shields-West, *The World Almanac of Presidential Campaigns*, 212.

66 Boller, *Presidential Campaigns*, 332.

66 Singer, *Campaign Speeches of American Presidential Candidates 1928–1972*, 358.

66 Ibid., 375.

67 Boller, *Presidential Campaigns*, 332.

71 *New York Times*, July 18, 1980, A8.

71 *New York Times*, August 15, 1980, B2.

71 Schlesinger, *Running for President*, 2:391.

75 Evan Thomas and Staff of *Newsweek, Election 2004: How Bush Won and What You Can Expect in the Future* (New York: Public Affairs, 2004), 49.

75 *New York Times*, August 18, 2000, A21.

75 *New York Times*, August 4, 2000, A24.

76 Jeffrey Toobin, *Too Close to Call: The Thirty-Six Day Battle to Decide the 2000 Election* (New York: Random House, 2001), 25.

78 *New York Times*, December 14, 2000, A26.

79 Michael Duffy and Karen Tumulty, "Coolness under Fire," *Time*, September 20, 2004, 25.

79 Ibid., 25.

79 Mike Allen, "President Launches Reelection Campaign," *Washington Post*, March 4, 2004, A04.

81 *Pittsburgh Post Gazette*, July 30, 2004, A8.

82 Historian's Office, *If Elected*, 261.

82 James Haskins, *Fighting Shirley Chisholm* (New York: Dial Press, 1975), 163.

SELECTED BIBLIOGRAPHY

The author also referenced biographies of each of the candidates, read through first-person accounts (diaries, letters, autobiographies, and newspaper clippings) and visited presidential homes.

Berkin, Carol, Christopher L. Miller, Robert W. Cherny, James L. Gormly, eds. *Making America: A History of the United States.* Boston: Houghton Mifflin Company, 1999.

Boller, Paul F., Jr. *Presidential Campaigns.* New York: Oxford University Press, 1984.

Boyer, Paul S., Clifford E. Clark Jr., Joseph F. Kett, Neal Salisbury, Harvard Sitkoff, and Nancy Woloch. *The Enduring Vision: A History of the American People.* Lexington, MA: D. C. Heath and Company, 1996.

Brinkley, Alan, and Davis Dyer, eds. *The Reader's Companion to the American Presidency.* Boston: Houghton Mifflin Company, 2000.

Cornog, Evan, and Richard Whelan. *Hats in the Ring: An Illustrated History of American Presidential Campaigns.* New York: Random House, 2000.

Davis, James W. *Springboard to the White House: Presidential Primaries: How They Are Fought and Won.* New York: Thomas Y. Crowell Company, 1967.

Graff, Henry F., ed. *The Presidents: A Reference History*. New York: Charles Scribner's Sons, 1984.

Historian's Office, National Portrait Gallery. *"If Elected...": Unsuccessful Candidates for the Presidency 1796–1968*. Washington, DC: Smithsonian Institution Press, 1972.

Kunhardt, Philip B., Jr., Philip B. Kunhardt III, and Peter W. Kunhardt. *The American President*. New York: Riverhead Books, 1999.

Matuz, Roger, and Lawrence W. Baker, eds. *Complete American Presidents Sourcebook*. Vols. 1–5. Detroit: UXL, 2001.

McPherson, James M., ed. *"To the Best of My Ability": The American Presidents*. New York: Dorling Kindersley, 2000.

Melder, Keith. *Hail to the Candidate: Presidential Campaigns from Banners to Broadcasts*. Washington, DC: Smithsonian Institution Press, 1992.

Norton, Mary Beth, David M. Katzman, Paul D. Escott, Howard P. Chudacoff, Thomas G. Paterson, and William M. Tuttle, Jr., eds. *A People and a Nation: A History of the United States*. Boston: Houghton Mifflin Company, 1998.

Porter, Kirk H., and Donald Bruce Johnson, eds. *National Party Platforms 1840–1964*. Urbana: University of Illinois Press, 1966.

Roseboom, Eugene H., and Alfred D. Eckes Jr. *A History of Presidential Elections: From George Washington to Jimmy Carter*. New York: Macmillan Publishing Co., 1979.

Schlesinger, Arthur M., Jr. *Running for President: The Candidates and Their Images, 1789–1896*. Vol. 1. New York: Simon & Schuster, 1994.

———. *Running for President: The Candidates and Their Images. 1900–1992*. Vol. 2, New York: Simon & Schuster, 1994.

———. *Selecting the President: From 1789 to 1996*. Washington, DC: Congressional Quarterly, 1997.

Shields-West, Eileen. *The World Almanac of Presidential Campaigns*. New York: World Almanac, 1992.

Singer, Aaron. *Campaign Speeches of American Presidential Candidates 1928–1972*. New York: Frederick Ungar Publishing Company, 1976.

Troy, Gil. *See How They Ran: The Changing Role of the Presidential Candidate*. New York: Free Press, 1991.

Urdang, Laurence, and Celia Dame Robbins. *Slogans*. Detroit: Gale Research Company, 1984.

Weisbord, Marvin R. *Campaigning for President: A Look at the Road to the White House*. New York: Washington Square Press, 1966.

Widmer, Ted. *Campaigns: A Century of Presidential Races*. New York: DK Publishing, 2001.

FURTHER READING AND WEBSITES

The Presidential Leaders series, published by Twenty-First Century Books (2003–2007) provides full-length biographies of U.S. presidents.

Bausum, Ann. *Our Country's Presidents*. Washington, DC: National Geographic, 2005.

Blassingame, Wyatt. *The Look-It-Up Book of Presidents*. New York: Random House, 2001.

Crompton, Samuel. *The Presidents of the United States*. New York: Smithmark Publishers, 1992.

Goldman, David J. *Presidential Losers*. Minneapolis: Lerner Publications Company, 2004.

Harvey, Miles. *Presidential Elections*. Chicago: Children's Press, 1995.

Henry, Christopher. *Presidential Elections*. New York: Franklin Watts, 1996.

Israel, Fred L. *Student's Atlas of American Presidential Elections 1789–1996*. Washington, DC: Congressional Quarterly, 1997.

Rubel, David. *Scholastic Encyclopedia of the Presidents and Their Times*. New York: Scholastic Reference, 2005.

Saffell, David C. *The Encyclopedia of U.S. Presidential Elections*. New York: Franklin Watts, 2004.

America Votes
http://scriptorium.lib.duke.edu/americavotes
This site has letters, posters, prints, buttons, photos, and more from the campaigns of John Adams to George W. Bush.

The Living Room Candidate
http://livingroomcandidate.movingimage.us/
This site contains video clips of campaign speeches and TV political ads from 1952 to 2004.

Presidential Campaigns
http://www.usconstitution.net/constop_pcam.html
This site includes information about how candidates are chosen and run for office. There is a glossary of terms, frequently asked questions, and articles of the Constitution that deal with elections.

Presidential Campaigns, Conventions, and Elections
http://www.presidentsusa.net/campaigns.html
This site contain detailed information about each campaign, the party conventions, and the results of every election.

INDEX

ACKNOWLEDGMENTS

The images in this book are used with the permission of: © Royalty-Free/CORBIS, p. 2; Independence National Historical Park, p. 6; Library of Congress, pp. 7 (LC-USZ62-2261), 10 (LC-USZ62-68224), 14 (LC-USZ62-89572), 18 (LC-USZ62-43901), 19 (LC-USZC4-970), 21 (LC-USZC4-12983), 23 (left) (LC-USZ62-40721), 23 (right) (LC-USZ62-96393), 27 (LC-USZ62-7561), 29 (LC-USZ62-40071), 31 (LC-USZ62-7490), 32 (LC-USZ62-132545), 34 (LC-USZC4-7997), 36 (LC-USZC2-2485), 39 (LC-USZ62-100971), 40 (LC-DIG-cwpbh-00554), 44 (LC-DIG-cwpbh-03668), 52 (LC-USZ62-41721), 53 (LC-USZ62-89631), 83 (LC-USZ62-84032), 98 (right) (LC-DIG-cwpbh-04374); © The Corcoran Gallery of Art/CORBIS, p. 16; © North Wind Picture Archives, pp. 25, 33; The Library of Virginia, p. 26; West Point Museum Art Collection, United States Military Academy, p. 38; Picture History, p. 42; President Benjamin Harrison Home Indianapolis, p. 46; Cincinnati Museum Center - Cincinnati Historical Society Library, p. 48; © Kean Collection/Hulton Archive/Getty Images, p. 50; © Brown Brothers, pp. 56, 58, 59, 61, 62, 64, 69; © Hulton Archive/Getty Images, p. 57, 98 (left); Franklin D. Roosevelt Library, p. 63; © Bettmann/CORBIS, pp. 67, 70, 78; © Cornell Capa/Time & Life Pictures/Getty Images, p. 68; National Archives, p. 72 (RG6S-KWP. 1458); Southdale-Hennepin Area Library, p. 75; Cecil Stoughton, White House/John Fitzgerald Kennedy Library, Boston, p. 76; © Julian Wasser/Time & Life Pictures/Getty Images, p. 79; © Lee Balterman/Time & Life Pictures/Getty Images, p. 80; AP Photo, p. 82; A 1979 Herblock Cartoon, copyright by The Herb Block Foundation. Image courtesy of the Prints & Photographs Division, Library of Congress, LC-USZ62-132513, p. 85; © David J. & Janice L. Frent Collection/CORBIS, p. 87; © Wally McNamee/CORBIS, p. 88; © Hector Mata/AFP/Getty Images, p. 90; © Erik Perel/AFP/Getty Images, p. 91; Gamble © 2000, The Florida Times-Union, p. 92; © Jeff Haynes/AFP/Getty Images, p. 96; © Michael Tighe/Hulton Archive/Getty Images, p. 99; © Diana Walker/Time & Life Pictures/Getty Images, p. 100; © Chris Hondros/Getty Images, p. 101 (left); © Darren Hauck/Getty Images, p. 101 (right).

Front Cover: Buttons: I Like Ike: © Todd Strand/Independent Picture Service; Clinton and Gore: © Todd Strand/Independent Picture Service; Reagan and Bush: © Todd Strand/Independent Picture Service; Kennedy and Johnson: © Todd Strand/Independent Picture Service; Harding and Coolidge: Library of Congress (LC-USZ62-95067); Nixon: From the collection of the Richard Nixon Library & Birthplace Foundation. Banners: Library of Congress, Cass and Butler, top left (LC-USZC2-585), Lincoln and Johnson, top right (LC-USZ62-14616), Grant and Colfax, bottom left, (LC-USZ62-92611), Taylor and Fillmore, bottom middle (LC-USZC2-584), Cleveland and Hendricks, bottom right (LC-DIG-pga-03158). Background: © Royalty-Free/CORBIS.

For more information, please call 1-800-328-4929 or visit www.lernerbooks.com